KARNATAKA

A STATE STUDY GUIDE

A.R. ANANTHAMURTHY

Published by

Hawk Press
4836/24, Ansari Road, Daryaganj
New Delhi – 110 002
Phones: 91-11-23278618, 91-11-43667199
E-mail: thehawkpress@gmail.com
www.thehawkpress.com

ISBN: 978-93-88318-77-8

Preface

Karnataka is a state in the south western region of India. It was formed on 1 November 1956, with the passage of the States Reorganisation Act. Originally known as the State of Mysore, it was renamed Karnataka in 1973. The state corresponds to the Carnatic region. The capital and largest city is Bangalore (Bengaluru).

Karnataka is one of the harbingers of socioeconomic and political changes in the country, particularly since 1991. Rural Karnataka is also showing welcome changes in agricultural, industrial and services sectors although the pace and pattern of these changes are not uniform. Karnataka, however, has some worrisome problems with regards to sectoral shifts. After a decade of reforms it is appropriate that an appraisal of these changes be made so that reprioritisation of the development initiatives can be done.

Karnataka is bordered by the Arabian Sea to the west, Goa to the northwest, Maharashtra to the north, Telangana to the northeast, Andhra Pradesh to the east, Tamil Nadu to the southeast, and Kerala to the south. The state covers an area of 191,976 square kilometres (74,122 sq mi), or 5.83 percent of the total geographical area of India. It is the seventh largest Indian state by area. With 61,130,704 inhabitants at the 2011 census, Karnataka is the eighth largest state by population, comprising 30 districts. Kannada, one of the classical languages of India, is the most widely spoken and official language of the state alongside Konkani, Marathi, Tulu, Tamil, Telugu, Malayalam, Kodava and Beary. Karnataka also has the only 3 naturally Sanskrit-speaking districts in India.

The two main river systems of the state are the Krishna

and its tributaries, the Bhima, Ghataprabha, Vedavathi, Malaprabha, and Tungabhadra, in the north, and the Kaveri and its tributaries, the Hemavati, Shimsha, Arkavati, Lakshmana Thirtha and Kabini, in the south. Most of these rivers flow out of Karnataka eastward, reaching the sea at the Bay of Bengal.

The diverse linguistic and religious ethnicities that are native to Karnataka, combined with their long histories, have contributed immensely to the varied cultural heritage of the state. Apart from Kannadigas, Karnataka is home to Tuluvas, Kodavas and Konkanis. Minor populations of Tibetan Buddhists and tribes like the Soligas, Yeravas, Todas and Siddhis also live in Karnataka.

The Government of Karnataka is a democratically elected body with the governor as the constitutional head. The governor who is appointed for five years appoints the chief minister and on the advice of the chief minister appoints his council of ministers. Even though the governor remains the ceremonial head of the state, the day-to-day running of the government is taken care of by the chief minister and his council of ministers in whom a great amount of legislative powers are vested.

Karnataka has a parliamentary system of government with two democratically elected houses, the Legislative Assembly and the Legislative Council. The Legislative Assembly consists of 224 members who are elected for five-year terms. The Legislative Council is a permanent body of 75 members with one-third (25 members) retiring every two years.

This is a reference book. All the matter is just compiled and edited in nature, taken from the various sources which are in public domain.

The book is intended to provide referral benefit to students, scholars and policy-makers.

—*Editor*

ABOUT THE BOOK

In India, Karnataka State stands first both in the area and production of Arecanut when compared to other states. In Karnataka among the 27 districts, Shimoga district stands first in area under areca cultivation more than 20,000 hectares in 2002. In addition to this, Shimoga district recorded the highest increase in area under Arecanut cultivation in the last decade (1990-91 to 2000-01) as compared to other districts. Karnataka is a state in the south western region of India. It was formed on 1 November 1956, with the passage of the States Reorganisation Act. Originally known as the State of Mysore, it was renamed Karnataka in 1973. The state corresponds to the Carnatic region. The capital and largest city is Bangalore (Bengaluru). The recorded history of Karnataka goes back more than two millennia. Several great empires and dynasties have ruled over Karnataka and have contributed greatly to the history, culture and development of Karnataka. Karnataka State has been divided into four revenue divisions, 49 sub-divisions, 30 districts, 176 taluks and 747 hoblies/revenue circles and 5628 gram panchayats for administrative purposes. The state has 281 towns and 7 municipal corporations. Bangalore is the fifth largest urban agglomeration out of 23 metropolis, urban agglomerations and cities in India. It is among the fastest growing cities in the world. The book is intended to provide referral benefit to students, scholars and policy-makers.

Contents

1

State at a Glance

Karnataka is a state in the south western region of India. It was formed on 1 November 1956, with the passage of the States Reorganisation Act. Originally known as the State of Mysore, it was renamed *Karnataka* in 1973. The state corresponds to the Carnatic region. The capital and largest city is Bangalore (Bengaluru).

Karnataka is bordered by the Arabian Sea to the west, Goa to the northwest, Maharashtra to the north, Telangana to the northeast, Andhra Pradesh to the east, Tamil Nadu to the southeast, and Kerala to the south. The state covers an area of 191,976 square kilometres (74,122 sq mi), or 5.83 percent of the total geographical area of India. It is the seventh largest Indian state by area. With 61,130,704 inhabitants at the 2011 census, Karnataka is the eighth largest state by population, comprising 30 districts. Kannada, one of the classical languages of India, is the most widely spoken and official language of the state alongside Konkani, Marathi, Tulu, Tamil, Telugu, Malayalam, Kodava and Beary. Karnataka also has the only 3 naturally Sanskrit-speaking districts in India.

The two main river systems of the state are the Krishna and its tributaries, the Bhima, Ghataprabha, Vedavathi, Malaprabha, and Tungabhadra, in the north, and the Kaveri and its tributaries, the Hemavati, Shimsha, Arkavati, Lakshmana Thirtha and Kabini, in the south. Most of these rivers flow out of Karnataka eastward, reaching the sea at the Bay of Bengal.

Though several etymologies have been suggested for the name Karnataka, the generally accepted one is that *Karnataka* is derived from the Kannada words *karu* and *nâdu*, meaning "elevated land". *Karu nadu* may also be read as *karu*, meaning "black", and *nadu*, meaning "region", as a reference to the black cotton soil found in the Bayalu Seeme region of the state. The British used the word Carnatic, sometimes *Karnatak*, to describe both sides of peninsular India, south of the Krishna.

HISTORY

Mallikarjuna temple and Kashi Vishwanatha temple at Pattadakal, built successively by the kings of the Chalukya Empire and Rashtrakuta Empire is a UNESCO World Heritage Site.

The economy of Karnataka is the fifth-largest state economy in India with 14.08 lakh crore (US$200 billion) in gross domestic product and a per capita GDP of 174,000 (US$2,400). With an antiquity that dates to the paleolithic, Karnataka has been home to some of the most powerful empires of ancient and medieval India. The philosophers and musical bards patronised by these empires launched socio-religious and literary movements which have endured to the present day. Karnataka has contributed significantly to both forms of Indian classical music, the Carnatic and Hindustani traditions.

Sala fighting the Lion, the emblem of Hoysala Empire

Statue of Ugranarasimha at Hampi, located within the ruins of Vijayanagara, the former capital of the Vijayanagara Empire

Karnataka's pre-history goes back to a paleolithic hand-axe culture evidenced by discoveries of, among other things, hand axes and cleavers in the region. Evidence of neolithic and megalithic cultures have also been found in the state. Gold discovered in Harappa was found to be imported from mines in Karnataka, prompting scholars to hypothesise about contacts between ancient Karnataka and the Indus Valley Civilisation ca. 3300 BCE.

Prior to the third century BCE, most of Karnataka formed part of the Nanda Empire before coming under the Mauryan empire of Emperor Ashoka. Four centuries of Satavahana rule followed, allowing them to control large areas of Karnataka. The decline of Satavahana power led to the rise of the earliest native kingdoms, the Kadambas and the Western Gangas, marking the region's emergence as an independent political entity. The Kadamba Dynasty, founded by Mayurasharma, had its capital at Banavasi; the Western Ganga Dynasty was formed with Talakad as its capital.

These were also the first kingdoms to use Kannada in administration, as evidenced by the Halmidi inscription and a fifth-century copper coin discovered at Banavasi. These dynasties were followed by imperial Kannada empires such as the Badami Chalukyas, the Rashtrakuta Empire of Manyakheta and the Western Chalukya Empire,which ruled over large parts of the Deccan and had their capitals in what is now Karnataka. The Western Chalukyas patronised a unique style of architecture and Kannada literature which became a precursor to the Hoysala art of the 12th century. Parts of modern-day Southern Karnataka (Gangavadi) were occupied by the Chola Empire at the turn of the 11th century. The Cholas and the Hoysalas fought over the region in the early 12th century before it eventually came under Hoysala rule.

At the turn of the first millennium, the Hoysalas gained power in the region. Literature flourished during this time, which led to the emergence of distinctive Kannada literary metres, and the construction of temples and sculptures adhering to the Vesara style of architecture. The expansion of the Hoysala Empire brought minor parts of modern Andhra Pradesh and Tamil Nadu under its rule. In the early 14th century, Harihara and Bukka Raya established the Vijayanagara empire with its capital, *Hosapattana* (later named Vijayanagara), on the banks of the Tungabhadra River in the modern Bellary district. The empire rose as a bulwark against Muslim advances into South India, which it completely controlled for over two centuries.

In 1565, Karnataka and the rest of South India experienced a major geopolitical shift when the Vijayanagara empire fell to a confederation of Islamic sultanates in the Battle of Talikota. The Bijapur Sultanate, which had risen after the demise of the Bahmani Sultanate of Bidar, soon took control of the Deccan; it was defeated by the Moghuls in the late 17th century. The Bahmani and Bijapur rulers encouraged Urdu and Persian literature and Indo-Saracenic architecture, the Gol Gumbaz being one of the high points of this style. During the sixteenth century, Konkani Hindus migrated to Karnataka, mostly from Salcette, Goa, while during the seventeenth and eighteenth century, Goan Catholicsmigrated to North Canara and South Canara, especially from Bardes, Goa, as a result of food shortages, epidemics and heavy taxation imposed by the Portuguese.

1792 Portrait of Tipu Sultan, kept at the British Library

In the period that followed, parts of northern Karnataka were ruled by the Nizam of Hyderabad, the Maratha Empire, the British, and other powers.In the south, the Mysore Kingdom, a former vassal of the Vijayanagara Empire, was briefly independent. With the death of Krishnaraja Wodeyar II, Haidar Ali, the commander-in-chief of the Mysore army, gained control of the region. After his death, the kingdom was inherited by his son Tipu Sultan. To contain European expansion in South India, Haidar Ali and later Tipu Sultan fought four significant Anglo-Mysore Wars, the last of which resulted in Tippu Sultan's death and the incorporation of Mysore into the British Raj in 1799. The Kingdom of Mysore was restored to the Wodeyars and Mysore remained a princely state under the British Raj.

As the "doctrine of lapse" gave way to dissent and resistance from princely states across the country, Kittur Chennamma, Sangolli Rayanna and others spearheaded rebellions in Karnataka in 1830, nearly three decades before the Indian Rebellion of 1857. However, Kitturu was taken over by the British East India Company even before the doctrine was officially articulated by Lord Dalhousie in 1848. Other uprisings followed, such as the ones at Supa, Bagalkot, Shorapur, Nargund and Dandeli. These rebellions — which coincided with the Indian Rebellion of 1857 – were led by Mundargi Bhimarao, Bhaskar Rao Bhave, the

Halagali Bedas, Raja Venkatappa Nayaka and others. By the late 19th century, the independence movement had gained momentum; Karnad Sadashiva Rao, Aluru Venkata Raya, S. Nijalingappa, Kengal Hanumanthaiah, Nittoor Srinivasa Rau and others carried on the struggle into the early 20th century.

After India's independence, the Maharaja, Jayachamarajendra Wodeyar, allowed his kingdom's accession to India. In 1950, Mysore became an Indian state of the same name; the former Maharaja served as its *Rajpramukh* (head of state) until 1975. Following the long-standing demand of the Ekikarana Movement, Kodagu- and Kannada-speaking regions from the adjoining states of Madras, Hyderabad and Bombay were incorporated into the Mysore state, under the States Reorganisation Act of 1956. The thus expanded state was renamed Karnataka, seventeen years later, in 1973. In the early 1900s through the post-independence era, industrial visionaries such as Sir Mokshagundam Visvesvarayya, born in Muddenahalli, Chikballapur district, played an important role in the development of Karnataka's strong manufacturing and industrial base.

HISTORY OF KARNATAKA

The recorded history of Karnataka goes back more than two millennia. Several great empires and dynasties have ruled over Karnataka and have contributed greatly to the history, culture and development of Karnataka.

The impact of kingdoms of Karnataka origin have been felt over other parts of India also. The Chindaka Nagas of central India, Gangas of Kalinga (Odisha), Rashtrakutas of Manyakheta, Chalukyas of Vengi, Yadava Dynasty of Devagiri were all of Kannada originwho later took to encouraging local languages.

Pre-history

The credit for doing early extensive study of prehistoric Karnataka goes to Robert Bruce-Foote and this work was later continued by many other scholars. The pre-historic culture of Karnataka (and South India in general) is called the hand-axe culture, as opposed to the Sohan culture of North India. Paleolithic hand axes and cleavers in the shape of pebbles made with quartz and quartzite which have been found in places such as Lingadahalli in Chikkamagaluru district and Hunasagi in Yadgir district, and a wooden spike at Kibbanahalli in Tumkur district are examples of old stone age implements.

There are reports that a polished stone axe was discovered at Lingasugur in the Raichur district Neolithic sites (new stone age) of importance are Maski in Raichur district, Brahmagiri in Chitradurga district etc., with abundance of evidence that man begun to domesticate animals such as cows, dogs and sheep, use copper and bronze weapons, wear bangles, rings, necklaces of beads and ear-rings and have burial chambers. To the end of the Neolithic era, during the Megalithic age, people in Karnataka began to use long swords, sickles, axes, hammers, spikes, chisels and arrows, all made of iron.

Scholarly hypothesis postulates contacts between the Indus Valley (3300 BCE - 1300 BCE) cities of Harappa and Lothal, citing the discovery of gold found in the Harappan sites that was imported from mines in Karnataka.

Evidence of Neolithic habitation of areas in modern Karnataka and celts dating back to the 2nd century BCE were first discovered in 1872. There are reports that a polished stone axe was discovered at Lingsugur in the Raichur district; however the authenticity of these reports remains unverifiable. Megalithic structures and burial grounds were discovered in 1862 in the regions of Kodagu and Moorey Betta hills, while Neolithic sites were discovered in north Karnataka. Scholarly hypothesis postulates of contacts between the Indus Valley city of Harappa in 3000 BCE, citing the discovery of gold found in the Harappan sites that was imported from mines in Karnataka.

Early history

Karnataka was the part of the Maurya Empire, the first Mauryan Emperor Chandragupta Maurya died in Shravanbelgola in Hassan Districtaround 298 BCE where he spent last days of his life as Jain ascetic.

Hoysala Empire architecture in Belur

Around 230 BCE, the Satavahana dynasty came to power and its rule lasted nearly four centuries, until the early 3rd century CE. The disintegration of the Satavahana dynasty led to the ascent of the earliest native kingdoms, the Kadamba Dynasty of Banavasi in modern Uttara Kannada district with Mayurasharma, a Brahmin native of Talagunda in modern Shivamogga district as the founding king, and the Western Ganga Dynasty in southern Karnataka, marking the birth of the region as an independent political entity. These were the first kingdoms to give administrative status to Kannada language as evidenced by the Halmidi inscription of 450, attributed to King Kakusthavarma of the Kadamba Dynasty. Also, recent discovery of a 5th-century copper coin in Banavasi, ancient capital of the Kadambas, with Kannada script inscription on it, further proves the usage of Kannada at an official level.

Medieval history

Bahubali statue in Shravanabelagola

They were followed by large imperial empires, the Badami Chalukyas, Rashtrakuta Dynasty and Western Chalukya Empire, who had their regal capitals in modern Karnataka region and patronised Kannada language and literature. Parts of Karnataka were conquered by the Chola Empire in the 11th century.

Natives of the malnad Karnataka, the Hoysalas established the Hoysala Empire at the turn of the first millennium. Art and architecture flourished in the region during this time resulting in distinctive Kannada literary metres and the construction of temples and sculptures adhering to the *Vesara*style of architecture. The expansion of the Hoysala Empire brought large parts of modern Andhra Pradesh and Tamil Nadu under their rule.

In the early 14th century, the Vijayanagara Empire with its capital at Hosapattana (later to be called Vijayanagara) rose to successfully challenge the Muslim invasions into the South. This empire was established by Harihara I and Bukka Raya who many historians claim were commanders of the last Hoysala King Veera Ballala III and the empire prospered for over two centuries.

Gol Gumbaz, tomb of Mohammed Adil Shah, seventh Sultan of Bijapur

The Bahmani sultans of Bidar were the main competitors to the Vijayanagara empire for hegemony over the Deccan and after their fall, the Bijapur Sultanate took their place in the dynastic struggle for control of the southern India. After the defeat and disintegration of the Vijayanagara Empire in battle at Talikota in 1565 to a confederacy of Sultanates, the Bijapur Sultanate rose as the main power in the Deccan before their defeat to the Mughal Empire in late 17th century. Mughal Emperor Aurangzeb gave the order to besiege Bijapur and after a 15-month long siege, the Mughal army emerged victorious and the Adil Shahi dynasty came to an end.

The Bahmani and Bijapur rulers encouraged Urdu and Persian literature and Indo Islamic architecture, the Gol Gumbaz being one of the high points of this contribution. Parts of Karnataka were conquered by Marathas, earlier under Chhatrapati Shivaji and later on after the War of 27 years.

Modern history

Mysore Palace

The Wodeyars of Mysore, former vassals of the Vijayanagara Empire, leased the state from the Mughal king Aurangzeb in the 17th century. With the death of Krishnaraja Wodeyar II, Haider Ali, the Commander-in-Chief of the Mysore Army, assumed control over the region, until the rule of the kingdom was passed to Tipu Sultan, after Haider Ali's death. In attempting to contain European expansion in South India, Tipu Sultan, known as the *Tiger of Mysore* fought four significant Anglo-Mysore Wars, the last of which resulted in his death and the incorporation of Mysore into the British Raj.

Unification of Karnataka

After Indian independence, the Wodeyar Maharaja acceded to India. In 1950, Mysore became an Indian state, and the former Maharaja became its *rajpramukh*, or governor, until 1975. The *Ekikarana* movement which started in the later half of the 20th century, culminated in the *States Reorganisation Act* of 1956 which provided for parts of Coorg, Madras, Hyderabad, and Bombay states to be incorporated into the state of Mysore. Mysore state was renamed *Karnataka* in 1973. The state of Mysore was formed on November 1, 1956 and since then November 1 of every year is celebrated as Kannada Rajyotsava / Karnataka Rajyotsava.

MEDIA

The era of Kannada newspapers started in the year 1843 when Hermann Mögling, a missionary from Basel Mission, published the first Kannada newspaper called *Mangalooru Samachara* in Mangalore. The first Kannada periodical, *Mysuru Vrittanta Bodhini* was started by Bhashyam Bhashyacharya in Mysore. Shortly after Indian independence in 1948, K. N. Guruswamy founded *The Printers (Mysore) Private Limited* and began publishing two newspapers, *Deccan Herald* and *Prajavani*. Presently the *Times of India* and *Vijaya Karnataka* are the largest-selling English and Kannada newspapers respectively. A vast number of weekly, biweekly and monthly magazines are under publication in both Kannada and English. *Udayavani*, *Kannadaprabha*, *Samyukta Karnataka*, *VarthaBharathi*, *Sanjevani*, *Eesanje*, *Hosa digantha*, *Karavali Ale* are also some popular dailies published from Karnataka.

Doordarshan is the broadcaster of the Government of India and its channel DD Chandana is dedicated to Kannada. Prominent Kannada channels include Colors Kannada, Zee Kannada and Udaya TV.

Karnataka occupies a special place in the history of Indian radio. In 1935, *Aakashvani*, the first private radio station in India, was started by Prof. M.V. Gopalaswamy in Mysore.The popular radio station was taken over by the local municipality and later by All India Radio (AIR) and moved to Bangalore in 1955. Later in 1957, AIR adopted the original name of the radio station, *Aakashavani* as its own. Some of the popular programs aired by AIR Bangalore included *Nisarga Sampada* and *Sasya Sanjeevini* which were programs that taught science through songs, plays and stories. These two programs became so popular that they were translated and broadcast in 18 different languages and the entire series was recorded on cassettes by the Government of Karnataka and distributed to thousands of schools across the state. Karnataka has witnessed a growth in FM radio channels, mainly in the cities of Bangalore, Mangalore and Mysore, which has become hugely popular.

SPORTS

Karnataka's smallest district, Kodagu, is a major contributor to Indian field hockey, producing numerous players who have represented India at the international level. The annual Kodava Hockey Festival is the largest hockey tournament in the world. Bangalore has hosted a WTA tennisevent and, in 1997, it hosted the fourth National Games of India. The Sports Authority of India, the premier sports institute in the country, and the Nike Tennis Academy are also situated in Bangalore. Karnataka has been referred to as the cradle of Indian swimming because of its high standards in comparison to other states.

One of the most popular sports in Karnataka is cricket. The state cricket team has won the Ranji Trophy seven times, second only to Mumbai in terms of success. Chinnaswamy Stadium in Bangalore regularly hosts international matches and is also the home of the National Cricket Academy, which was opened in 2000 to nurture potential international players. Many cricketers have represented India and in one international match held in the 1990s; players from Karnataka composed the majority of the national team. The Royal Challengers Bangalore, an Indian Premier League franchise, the Bengaluru Football

Club, an Indian Super League franchise, the Bengaluru Yodhas, a Pro Wrestling League franchise, the Bengaluru Blasters, a Premier Badminton League franchise and the Bengaluru Bulls, a Pro Kabaddi League franchise are based in Bangalore. The Karnataka Premier League is an inter-regional Twenty20 cricket tournament played in the state.

Notable sportsmen from Karnataka include B.S. Chandrasekhar, Anil Kumble, Javagal Srinath, Rahul Dravid, Venkatesh Prasad, Robin Uthappa, Vinay Kumar, Gundappa Vishwanath, Syed Kirmani, Stuart Binny, Ashwini Ponnappa, Mahesh Bhupathi, Rohan Bopanna, Prakash Padukone who won the All England Badminton Championships in 1980 and Pankaj Advani who has won three world titles in cue sports by the age of 20 including the amateur World Snooker Championship in 2003 and the World Billiards Championship in 2005.

Bijapur district has produced some of the best known road cyclists in the national circuit. Premalata Sureban was part of the Indian contingent at the Perlis Open '99 in Malaysia. In recognition of the talent of cyclists in the district, the state government laid down a cycling track at the B.R. Ambedkar Stadium at a cost of 40 lakh.

Sports like *kho kho*, *kabaddi*, *chinni daandu* and *goli* (marbles) are played mostly in Karnataka's rural areas.

2

Culture and Society

CULTURE

The diverse linguistic and religious ethnicities that are native to Karnataka, combined with their long histories, have contributed immensely to the varied cultural heritage of the state. Apart from Kannadigas, Karnataka is home to Tuluvas, Kodavas and Konkanis. Minor populations of Tibetan Buddhists and tribes like the Soligas, Yeravas, Todas and Siddhis also live in Karnataka.

The traditional folk arts cover the entire gamut of music, dance, drama, storytelling by itinerant troupes, etc. *Yakshagana* of Malnad and coastal Karnataka, a classical dance drama, is one of the major theatrical forms of Karnataka.

Contemporary theatre culture in Karnataka remains vibrant with organisations like *Ninasam*, *Ranga Shankara*, *Rangayana* and *Prabhat Kalavidaru*continuing to build on the foundations laid by Gubbi Veeranna, T. P. Kailasam, B. V. Karanth, K V Subbanna, Prasanna and others.

Veeragase, *Kamsale*, *Kolata* and *Dollu Kunitha* are popular dance forms. The Mysorestyle of *Bharatanatya*, nurtured and popularised by the likes of the legendary Jatti Tayamma, continues to hold sway in Karnataka, and Bangalore also enjoys an eminent place as one of the foremost centres of *Bharatanatya*.

A yakshagana *artist*

Karnataka also has a special place in the world of Indian classical music, with both Karnataka (Carnatic) and Hindustani styles finding place in the state, and Karnataka has produced a number of stalwarts in both styles. The Haridasa movement of the sixteenth century contributed significantly to the development of Karnataka (Carnatic) music as a performing art form. Purandara Dasa, one of the most revered Haridasas, is known as the *Karnataka Sangeeta Pitamaha* ('Father of Karnataka a.k.a. Carnatic music'). Celebrated Hindustani musicians like Gangubai Hangal, Mallikarjun Mansur, Bhimsen Joshi, Basavaraja Rajaguru, Sawai Gandharva and several others hail from Karnataka, and some of them have been recipients of the Kalidas Samman, Padma Bhushan and Padma Vibhushan awards. Noted Carnatic musicians include Violin T. Chowdiah, Veena Sheshanna, Mysore Vasudevachar, Doreswamy Iyengar and Thitte Krishna Iyengar.

Gamaka is another classical music genre based on Carnatic music that is practised in Karnataka. *Kannada Bhavageete* is a genre of popular music that draws inspiration from the expressionist poetry of modern poets. The Mysore school of painting has produced painters like Sundarayya, Tanjavur

Kondayya, B. Venkatappa and Keshavayya. *Chitrakala Parishat* is an organisation in Karnataka dedicated to promoting painting, mainly in the Mysore painting style.

Saree is the traditional dress of women in Karnataka. Women in Kodagu have a distinct style of wearing the *saree*, different from the rest of Karnataka. *Dhoti*, known as *Panche* in Karnataka, is the traditional attire of men. Shirt, Trousers and *Salwar kameez* are widely worn in Urban areas. *Mysore Peta* is the traditional headgear of southern Karnataka, while the *pagadi* or *pataga* (similar to the Rajasthani turban) is preferred in the northern areas of the state.

Rice and *Ragi* form the staple food in South Karnataka, whereas *Jolada rotti*, Sorghum is staple to North Karnataka. *Bisi bele bath*, *Jolada rotti*, *Ragi mudde*, *Uppittu*, *Benne Dose*, *Masala Dose* and *Maddur Vade* are some of the popular food items in Karnataka. Among sweets, *Mysore Pak*, *Karadantu* of Gokak and *Amingad*, *Belgaavi Kunda* and *Dharwad pedha* are popular. Apart from this, coastal Karnataka and Kodagu have distinctive cuisines of their own. Udupi cuisine of coastal Karnataka is popular all over India.

CUISINE OF KARNATAKA

Among food, South Karnataka people take Ragi Mudde along with Sambar, incase of veg, muddhe has good combination with dal like bassaru, sappina saru, etc. Similarly in case of nonveg, muddhe is a must for south karnataka persons. For north karnataka, jolada rotti (Jowar Roti) has a good combination with Kempu (Red) chutney and Ucchel chutney). Places like Udupi and Kodagu like dishes of Dosa, Idli, Bonda. Mangaluru peoples worship Fish as god, their usual dish is Fish along with Rice. The cuisine of Karnataka includes many vegetarian and non-vegetarian cuisines. It is one of the oldest surviving cuisines and traces its origin to the Iron Age. Ragi is mentioned in the historical works of the great poet Adikavi Pampa and in the ancient Sanskrit medical text Sushruta Samhita. The varieties of the Karnataka cuisine have drawn influence from and influenced the cuisines of neighbouring states like Tamil Nadu, Andhra Pradesh and Kerala. Some typical dishes include Bisi bele bath, Jolada rotti, Chapati, Ragi rotti, Akki rotti, Saaru, Idli - Vada Sambar, Vangi Bath, *Khara Bath, Kesari Bath,* Benne dose, Neer Dose, Ragi unda, Paddu (Gundponglu), Koli Saaru (chicken curry - Kannada style), Maamsa Saaru (Mutton Curry - Kannada style), and Uppittu. The well-known Masala Dosa traces its origin to Udupi cuisine. Plain and rava idli, Mysore Masala Dosa and Maddur Vade are popular in South Karnataka. Kodagu (Coorg) district is famous for spicy varieties of pork curries while coastal Karnataka boasts of many tasty seafood specialities. Among sweets, Mysore Pak, Holige, Obbattu, Dharwad pedha, Kunda, Chiroti, Sajjige, Kadabu/ Karjikaayi are well known.

Although the ingredients differ from one region to another, a typical Kannadiga Oota (Kannadiga meal) includes the following dishes in the order specified and is served on a banana leaf: Uppu (salt), *Kosambari,* Pickle, Palya, Gojju, Raita, dessert, Thovve, Chitranna, rice, and ghee.

After ghee is served to everyone, one may start the meal. This step is taken to ensure that everyone seated has been served completely.

What follows next is a series of soup-like dishes such as Saaru, Muddipalya, Majjige Huli or Kootu, eaten with hot rice. Gojju or Raita is served next, then two or three desserts are served, and finally, fried dishes such as Aambode or Bonda are served. The meal is completed with a serving of curd rice.

There is some diversity in the core food habits of North and South Karnataka. While northern-style dishes have jola and rice as the primary cereals, the south uses ragi and rice.

North Karnataka cuisine

The North Karnataka cuisine can be primarily found in the northern districts of Karnataka which include Dharwad, Bijapur, Gulbarga, Belgaum, Bidar, Yadgir, Bagalkot, Raichur, Davangere, Gadag, Haveri, Koppal and western and northern areas of Bellary. The cuisine is also considered a specialty in the cities of Southern Karnataka including Bengaluru, Tumakuru and Mysuru, with several restaurants offering this cuisine to meet the growing demand.

North Karnataka meal

The following is the typical menu of a vegetarian Northern Karnataka meal:

- *Jolada rotti.* Thin flatbread usually made from Jowar flour, baked on a fire or an iron skillet. Bajra and wheat flour is also used as an alternative.
- *Enne-gai / Tumbu-gai* - Small *badane kaayi* (aubergine) bulbs stuffed with dry stuffing including ground peanut, ground sesame, ginger, garlic, garam masala and salt, then sauteed with onions and other spices. Aubergine is also substituted with any other suitable vegetable.
- Popular sweets and desserts are Shenga undeand godi hugg
- *Peanut / Sesame chutney.* A variety of powder/dry chutney made from ground peanut or sesame.
- *Kempu Khaara,* also called "Ranjaka" - chutney paste made with/of red chillis, consumed as a condiment
- Kosambari

- *Bele or kaalu palya dal*, whole or sprouted *kadale, hesaru* (mung bean), *Lentils*, cooked with greens such as methi, spinach, dill and scallion, and sauteed with onions, ginger, garlic and other spices.
- *Raita bajji* - salad made from yogurt
- Raw Salads - of scallion, onion, green chili, methi leaves, sometimes with *oggaraNe* of sasive or jeerige
- *Anna* (Rice)
- Saaru - Lentil soup made with pepper, cumin, coriander seeds, asafoetida, tomatoes or tamarind.
- Papadum
- Dahi (yogurt) and buttermilk
- Butter or ghee
- Jhunka or Pitla - salty masala cakes made from Channa Dal powder
- Raw greens - spinach, methi (fenugreek), and hakkarike (arugula)
- Raw vegetables - radish, cucumber, onions, carrots, green chilis etc.

South Karnataka cuisine

The South Karnataka or old Mysuru region (also known as Bayaluseeme or the plains) includes the present-day Kolara, Bengaluru, Mysuru, Tumakuru, Mandya, Haasana, Chamarajanagara. Ragi and rice are the most important staple grains, Jowar and bajra are also cultivated and consumed in the drier parts of the region. The first meal of the day is breakfast, which is quite substantial. Regular meals consists of Ragi mudde or steamed dumpling made from ragi flour, a curry to roll bits of the dumpling often called Saaru, rice and yogurt. Optional accompaniments include a salad called Kosambari, various Palyas (fried, boiled or sauteed spicy vegetables) and assorted pickles.

Formal vegetarian meals are usually served in a particular order and required to be consumed in a particular order as well. These meals are served on Plantain leaves or Mutuka leaves, dry Tendu-like leaves staples together into big circular discs. First accompaniments are served which includes a variety of Palya, Kosambari, sweet-savory gojju, hot spicy chutney pickles, bajji, bonda, vade, Papads. The first course alternates between sweets and rice preparation. The second course is a set of curries to be consumed with rice. It generally starts with Tovve, a mild lentil dish laced with ghee, Majjige Huli, vegetables simmered in a mild yogurt sauce, followed by Huli, lentils and vegetables spiced and tempered with ghee, mustard, asafoetida and curry leaves. This is followed by tili Saaru, which is a thin lentil stock, spiced and laced with ghee and curry leaves. The final course of the meal is rice and curd with pickles. Buttermilk is also served to be consumed at the end of the meal. Mysuru is also famous for its sweet "Mysur Pak", made of milk, sugar, ghee and gram flour.

The hilly district of Kodagu (Coorg) also has its own unique cuisine which includes spicy meat (Pandi (Pork) Curry, chicken, mutton), Kadumbutt (round balls made of rice), Paputt, Thaliyaputt. The spicy meat curries derives a tangy taste from Kokum Kachampuli.

Karnataka cuisine - common to all regions

Some common vegetarian dishes prepared on a regular basis are:

Capsicum and paneer pulao with yogurt

Rice dishes

- Bisi bele bath - rice cooked with lentils, vegetables and spices; like huli with rice, but often richer
- Vaangi baath - cooked rice mixed with eggplant cooked in oil and spices; the eggplant is usually cooked into a palya beforehand and the vaangi baath mixed before serving
- Chitranna - cooked rice flavoured with spices, particularly oil-popped mustard seeds and turmeric
- Mosaranna - curd rice sometimes given a fried spicy touch with fried lentils and oil-popped mustard seeds.
- Puliyogare - cooked rice flavoured with spicy tamarind paste
- Maavinkaayi chitranna - cooked rice flavoured with raw green mango and spices
- Nimbekaayi chitranna - cooked rice flavoured with lemon and spices
- Avalakki - Akki (means rice), Avalakki is baked flat rice that is soaked briefly and stir fried with cumin seeds, turmeric powder, peanuts, onions, green chilies, garnished with shredded coconuts and cilantro leaves.
- Mandakki - Puffed rice that is soaked briefly and stir fried with cumin seeds, turmeric powder, peanuts, roasted ground grams, onions, green chilies, garnished with shredded coconuts and cilantro leaves.

Dosas

- Benne dose or butter dose - originating from central Karnataka city of Davangere
- Mysore masala dosa
- Set dosa - Thick pancakes made of rice batter garnished with a hint of coriander leaves, grated carrot and coconut, served with saagu and coconut chutney
- Saagu masala dosa - dosa stuffed with saagu

- Masala dosa (butter and non-butter variants) - inside of the dosa is smeared with red chutney made of onion, red chili and garlic; stuffed with Aloo gadde palya (made of potato and onion)
- Godhi dôse or dôsa made from wheat
- Ragi dôse or dôsa made from ragi
- Rave dôse or dôsa made from rave

Breads

- Ragi rotti - A flat thick pancake made with ragi dough and flavoured with chillies and onions; the dough is shaped and flattened by hand.
- Akki rotti - A thick, flat pancake-like dish made with a dough of rice flour, chillies, onions and salt; the dough is shaped and flattened by hand.
- Jolada rotti - A flat pancake dish made with a dough of Sorghum flour and salt; the dough is shaped and flattened by hand. Jowar may be sometimes replaced with bajra.
- Ragi unda- Steamed dumplings made by adding ragi flour to boiling water.
- Gunpangalu - Also known as Gundupongla, Mane Kaavali (skillet with houses), or Poddu. It is made with a rice

batter (similar to dose) and cooked in a special skillet with compartments.

- Sajje rotti/Bhakri - A thick, flat pancake-like dish made with a dough of pearl millet flour and salt; the dough is shaped and flattened by hand and sprinkled with sesame seeds

Chutneys

- Kadalekaayi chutney - roasted peanuts/groundnuts ground with dry red chilies . May have garlic and be tempered with hot oil fried mustard and curry leaves
- Hurali chutney
- Kaayi chutney - grated coconut ground with dal (kadale) salted and garnished with oil-fried mustard and curry leaves
- Kaayi chutney (green) - grated coconut ground with dal, green chillies and coriander salted and garnished with oil-fried mustard and curry leaves
- Kaayi chutney (red) - grated coconut chutney ground with dal and dried red chillies salted and garnished with oil-fried mustard and curry leaves
- Maavina chutney - grated raw green mango ground with grated coconut, dal, salted and garnished oil-fried mustard and curry leaves.
- Heerekai chutney - grated ridge-gourd peel ground with grated coconut, dal, salted and garnished oil-fried mustard and curry leaves.
- Eerulli chutney - grated onion peel ground with grated coconut, dal, salted and garnished oil-fried mustard and curry leaves.
- Uddina Bele chutney - fried Black Gram Dal with Tamarind, Red Chillies, salted and garnished oil-fried mustard and curry leaves.
- Pudina chutney - fried pudina leaves along onion, groundnut, black gram, green chilli, tamrind. Add sugar and grind to fine paste.

Palya or side dishes

- Hurali kaayi palya
- Hurali palya
- Hurali happala
- Badnekaayi palya
- Bendekaayi palya
- Allugade palya
- Ballekaayi palya

Kosambari

A salad prepared using simple ingredients such as lentils, green chillies and finely chopped coriander. The dish is generally finished with a tempering of mustard seeds and asafoetida. Common variants include kosambari made with the above ingredients in addition to grated cucumber or carrot.

Sweet and spicy dishes

- Menasinakaayi gojju
- HuNuse gojju - made with tamarind
- Bendekaayi gojju - boiled okra (ladyfinger) cooked in a gravy sweetened with jaggery and soured with tamarind.
- Tomato gojju - cooked cut or mashed tomato with a sweet-sour gravy.
- Eerulli (Onion) and Tomato gojju - cooked cut or mashed tomato mixed with cut onion with a sweet-sour gravy.
- Haagalakaayi gojju - Bittergourd pieces marinated with salt and turmeric to remove some bitterness cooked with a sweet and sour gravy.
- Thondekaayi gojju

Saaru (Gravy)

See also: Saaru

- Huli- Combination of vegetables and lentils simmered with spices, coconut, tamarind and seasoned with Ghee, asafoetida, curry leaves and mustard, it is an integral part of every formal meal.

- Majjige Huli- Cooked vegetables simmered in yogurt with coconut, spices, asafoetida, curry leaves and mustard.
- Tovve- Mushy lentils cooked till creamy, spiked with spices and Ghee. Vegetables are also added to this dish like Ridged gourd, cucumber etc.
- Obbatinna saaru - made from the left over broth while preparing the sweet obbattu.
- Bas saaru - made from the broth of boiled lentils and spring beans
- Mosoppinna - made from lentils and spinach
- Maskai- Combination of vegetables cooked and mashed with spices and seasoning.
- Menasina saaru - rasam made from pepper, turmeric, and other spices
- Bele saaru - has toor dal as one of the ingredients
- Kaalina saaru - Legumes cooked with coconut, spices, tamarind and tempered with asafoetida, curry leaves and mustard. Popular legumes include Kadale kaalu or Chickpeas, Halasande Kaalu black-eyed peas, Hesaru kaalu moong beans, Hurali kaalu Horse gram, Avare kaalu Indian beans
- Haagalakaayi saaru - Haagalakai, the Indian bitter gourd is simmered with coconut, tamarind and spices and spiked with jaggery and asafoetida, curry leaves and mustard The bitterness of the gourd is cut through by the sweetness of the jaggery and tartness of the tamarind.
- Gojju- traditionally this is thicker than the Saaru but thinner than chutney. It is served with hot rice and is sweet, tangy and spicy. It is served in between courses as a palate cleanser. It is made from diverse ingredients including eggplants, okra, fenugreek, tamarind, pineapple, bitter gourd, tomatoes, lemon-lime, etc.
- Udaka- traditionally made in Chitradurga district only, served with Ragi ball. made from boiling lentils & green leaves, then broth taken separate from lentil/herbs leaves with chatney herbs & spices then mixed with broth.

- Tambuli - A yogurt based cold dish similar to Raita made from Doddapatre soppu. Optional ingredients in this dish includes vegetables and greens.
- Fish / Mutton / Chicken Saaru - A very famous local curry made mainly from assorted spices and meats. Often mixed and eaten with Ragi unda and rice or Bhakri

Sweets

- Huggi - cooked rice and kadale or *hesaru* (mung bean), with coconut, milk, elakki and sweetened with bella (jaggery)
- Ginnu - sweetened, flavoured and steam boiled colostrum of cow, buffalo or goat
- Kajjaya - Rice and jaggery fritters deep fried in Ghee.
- Kadabu - deep fried (kari kadubu) or steamed pastry with assorted sweet filling.
- Karjikaayi - deep fried crisp pastry with dry sweet filling
- Unde - ball shaped sweets with the following variations :

Chikkina unde - ellu and bella

Chigali unde - made from ellu

Rrave unde - made from semolina

Shenga unde - made from peanut

Mandakki unde - made from mandakki

avalakki unde - made from avalakki

Hesarunde Moong dal ladoo.

Godhiunde- made from Wheat

Gulaadike Unde- made from Maida and Sugar - A Davangere speciality,

Besanunde - made from besan

Tambittu - made from rice or wheat flour and jaggery.

Sikkinunde - made from jaggery, dried coconut and maida.

- Sakkare achhu - little sugar statues/toys made during Sankranti

- Haalubaayi - A fudge made with ground rice, jaggery and coconut.
- Mysore pak- A fudge made with Chickpea flour, sugar and ghee.
- Dharwad pedha- Milk scalded and thickened with sugar. Synonymous with Dharwad
- Karadantu - Gokak town in Belgaum district and Amingarh of Hunagunda Taluk in Bagalkot district of Karnataka is famous for the karadantu, the most famous form has a mixture of dry fruits and edible gum.
- Sheekarani - pulp of ripe fruit (usually mango or banana) with additions such as sugar, elakki, jaakayi, jaapatri, milk, etc.
- Damrottu - Ash gourd toasted in ghee and simmered with sugar, milk solids and sweet spices
- Kunda - prepared from thickened milk, a specialty from BeLagaavi
- Senige Huggi - A very famous sweet made during Diwali in Shikaripur near Shimoga
- Sweet Pastries - The following can be grouped together. These are often accompanied by milled sugar or warm milk flavoured with saffron and almonds.

Mandige - huge flat leavened pastry. It is quite a treat to watch chefs making large (>36 inches in diameter) pastries with bare hands and baking them on upturned clay pots over fire.

This is an ancient dish mentioned in a few inscriptions as the Sanskritised *mandaka*. For instance, a Western Chalukya inscription of A.D. 1121 mentions that Govinda-Dandadhipa, a famous general of Vikramaditya VI, is said to have made a provision for offering this dish as *naivedya* to Brahma, Vishnu and Maheshvara, at Pauthage.

Chiroti, phenori - unleaved, layered, sugar-coated fried sweets.

Shaavige chiroti - vermicelli pastry.

- Kesaribhath, Sira - This is made of rice (or semolina in southern Karnataka) cooked with sugar/jaggery, cardamom, saffron, milk, dry fruits (mostly raisins), and sometimes fresh fruits like banana, mango and pineapple. Popularly colored yellow/orange/saffron or left white. In North Karnataka, the semolina version is called *Sihi Sajjige* or *Sheera* or *Sira*; kesaribhath usually refers to the rice version.
- Hayagreeva - A chickpea based dessert prepared on special occasions; popular amongst the Maadhwa community
- Paramanna - Rice pudding with ghee and jaggery
- Mamu Puri - Flour, ghee, sugar, Khoa, first khoa is packed between 2 halves of chapati then fried. It is exported mainly to gulf.
- Maaldi - A delicious sweet dish made of powdered 'baked wheat roti's', poppy seed, jaggery, *hurakadle* (daria), and served with ghee. It is a must sweet on the occasion of marriages .

Pickles

Pickles are usually raw seasoned vegetables and sea food, but there are cooked varieties as well called Bisi Uppinakayi (hot pickle). The seasoning varies from plain salt to spices like green chilli, red chilli powder, black pepper, whole and powdered mustard seeds, coriander seeds, etc. They significantly differ from North Indian pickles or achar in that considerably less oil is usually used in the pickles; salt is the main preservative.

- Mavinkayi - Raw green mango
- Midi Mavinkaayi - Immature raw mangoes, usually used whole
- Amtekayi
- Nimbekayi - Whole and sliced lemon and lime
- Gaja Nimbekayi - A larger variety of lemon, resembling a grapefruit
- Bettada Nellikayi

- Nellikayi
- Tomato
- Heralikayi - a green citrus fruit, only the peel is used in the pickle.
- Hagalakayi - bitter gourd
- Prawn, shrimp and crab, especially in coastal areas
- Avakaya
- Avarekai

Snacks

- Churumuri
- Pakoda
- Vadey - Ambode, Sabbakki vadey, Bele vadey etc.

Sabakki vade

- Chakkuli

Chakli in hot oil

- Nippattu
- Nuchchina Unde
- Kodubale
- Khaara Mandakki - Puffed rice mixed with Khara (commonly called as a mixture), onions, green chilies, coriander, dash of lemon and salt.
- Aalugadde Bonda - A bonda made by deep frying lightly seasoned boiled mashed potato dipped in chickpea batter.
- Nargis Mandakki - A puffed rice dish popular in central and north Karnataka, especially in Devanagari district.
- Menasin kai bajji - Green chilli bajji, popular across the state of Karnataka.
- Dappa menasin kai bonda - Capsicum bonda.
- Baaley Kai Bajji - Raw unripe Banana bajji.
- Baalaka - deep fried vegetable and fruit chips or wafers. The vegetables are usually dried and seasoned with spices, and even butter milk. Common candidates are potato, sweet potato, yam, cassava, ripe jack fruit, banana,

plantain, chilli, bitter gourd, varieties of suitable green bean pods (usually *gori kaayi/chaLLe kaayi*), etc.

- Chigali (Hunase/Tamarind Chigali)

Udupi cuisine

Udupi cuisine takes its name from Udupi, a city on west coast of Karnataka. Udupi cuisine has its origin in Ashta mathas of Udupi founded by Shri Madhvacharya. Its core is a vast range of creative dishes emphasizing local vegetables and fruits.

Malenadu cuisine

The Malenadu of Karnataka can be culturally divided (on basis of food culture) as South Malnad comprising Northern Somawarpete in North Kodagu, Sakaleshapura, Mudigere, southern part of Chickamagaluru taluk and western part of Belur and Alur taluks in Hassan. Central Malnad consisting of Chickamagalur, Koppa and the Malnad region of Shivmoga, and western ghat regions of Uttara Kannada. Even though Western ghat regions of Uttara knnada and Belagavi can be considered as Northern malnad the food culture of these regions is unaware to the rest of Malnad, which may be due to inadequate communication with the other areas of Malnad and Karnataka. Although many refer to the Malenadu cuisine as an amalgam of Coorgi and Mangalorean cuisine, it has its own distinct style. The Kodava (Coorg) and the Bunt(coastal Mangalorean) regions are distinct from the rest of the Malnad region. The word *Malenaadu* means "land of mountain ranges". The cuisine is heavily influenced by the variety of fruits and vegetables available in the rich forests of western ghats. The ingredients like tender bamboo shoots, colocassia leaves, turmeric leaves, and raw jackfruit are easily found in the Sahyadri ranges. Steaming is the favored method of cooking in Malenaadu. More often than not, there is little use of oils in Malenaadu cuisine.

- Kaalu kadabu – small kadubus (dumplings) as small as kaalu (beans) made by pounding water-washed rice into powder and then steamed to make it sticky enough to make dumplings. Once the kadubus (thousands in number) are made is given typical malnad masale (red chili, oil, mustard, graped coconut, jeera, little tamrind juice, curry leaves, salt to taste, etc.) and served hot with hot thuppa (homemade ghee from cow's or buffalo's milk). Prepared around the region of Hanubalu, in Sakaleshpura taluk of Hassan district.

- Chattituttu – An evening snack usually prepared by grinding rice with other ingredients such as chili, salt, coconut and tiny square sliced onions are added to make a thick mixture. Which then will be spread (1/2 inch to 3/4 inch thick and approximately 6 inches in diameter) over thoroughly oiled bisi henchu (hot tava) once it becomes hard enough, kenda (burning charcoal) will be placed over it to crisp it. Prepared around the region of Hanubalu, in Sakaleshpura taluk of Hassan district.
- Kotte kadabu
- Kadabu
- Chicken saaru
- Chicken fry
- Voththu Shaavige with chicken curry
- Voththu shaavige with ghasghase paayasa or kaayi haalu – Steamed rice noodles with a sweet payasa or sweetened coconut milk
- Votthushaavige uppittu – Steamed rice noodles stir fried with oil, mustard seeds, onions, green chillies and curry leaves
- Akki rotti – rice rotti or flat bread made with rice
- Bamboo shoot pickle – Kalule' uppinakayi
- Bamboo shoot curry – Kalule' palya
- Halasina haNinna kadabu, paayasa
- Halasina haNinna happla
- Maavina midi uppinnakkayi
- Halasina haNinna dose - jackfruit dose
- Akki Tari Kadabu – breakfast dish made with broken rice
- Gangala dose – steamed dosa

- Angu or Thode-daaga – very thin sweet crepe made with a thin batter of rice and jaggery
- Kaayi Holige – a dessert made with fresh coconut, jaggery and maida
- Haalu Payasa – rice pudding, falvored with turmeric leaves and cardamom
- Haalu Hittu - semi-soft milk pudding made with milk, rice paste and sugar
- Kesina Soppina Palya – A side dish prepared using colocasia leaves as the main ingredient, served with akki rotti
- Kesuvina gantu- A dish made by rolling tender colocassia leaves and making a gantu (knot) sometimes a single hunk of rock salt and a garlic petal will be placed inside. The gantu should be tight enough that it should not open while steaming. The steamed gantus are given little touch of tamrind juice and chilli. Can be consumed with akki rotti, rice, chapathi. Or just as it is.[Again a dish prepared in the region of Hanbalu in Sakaleshpura].
- Thumbuli – a cool saaru usually made in summer using yogurt, ginger, pepper and other spices. Served with steamed rice.
- Maaldi – a coarse cereal made from ground whole wheat, jaggery, black til and other ingredients. Usually served in a bowl with either milk or ghee.
- Aralu pudi - a rice cereal made of ground toasted or puffed rice, jaggery, Elaichi are pounded to powder thin. Usually served in a bowl with warm milk. This cereal is also used as a filling in a special dessert called hurulu kadabu.
- Hoorulu kadabu - A traditional dessert made with aralu pudi, jaggery, coconut and other ingredients. The mixture is shaped and steamed in turmeric leaves.
- Kaadu mavinahannina saaru – a sweet and sour saaru made with whole tiny ripe mangoes. Served with cooked rice.

- Kaapi-Coffee- fresh grounded, filtered coffee well mixed with thick milk and sugar. It's served at least five to six times a day in coffee growing regions of Malnad such as Somawarapete, Sakaleshapura, Mudigere, Chickamagaluru taluk and western part of Belur and Alur taluks in Hassan.

Kodagu cuisine

Kodagu's staple food is rice. Traditional dishes include

- Pandi curry or pork curry
- Kadambuttu or steamed rice dumplings
- Koli saaru or chicken curry
- Bimbale curry or Bamboo shoot curry
- Paputtu or steamed rice cake
- Nool puttu and koli curry

North Canara (Coastal/Malenadu Karnataka) cuisine

Uttara Kannada (North Canara) is known for a variety of seafood delicacies. The staple diet includes a portion of steamed rice and a vegetable and/or seafood accompaniment. Seafood is immensely popular due to its ease of availability, and is prepared with a lot of local spices. Tea is the most popular beverage and is sometimes supplemented with cardamom or mint to give them a distinct flavour.

- Kadubu: The main ingredients are jackfruit pulp and jaggery. The batter is prepared and, with additional ingredients, the batter is put into a container and steamed. The dessert is a local delicacy and is served hot with ghee.
- Holige: These are stuffed wheat flour flatbreads. One variant is made with gram flour and jaggery, which is similar to the Puran poli of Maharashtra. The other variant is made with a coconut based filling.
- Todadevu: is a special kind of thin-crust dosa made out of jaggery or sugarcane juice. (Most local desserts of Sirsi have jaggery rather than sugar.)

- Kesaribath: is rice cooked in sugar, ghee, and kesari.
- Karakali: is a special kind of chutney which tastes very spicy. It is prepared from colocasia leaves.
- Kotte Roti: A form of idli-like preparation, steam cooked in a conical shaped container constructed using jackfruit leaves.
- Patrode : a special dish prepared by steaming stuffed colocasia leaves.
- Neer Dose: A soft thin pancake made of batter of boiled rice, coconut milk and salt
- Kajmiji
- Koli Kajjaya and Hosagere Kajjaya are made of rice flour and fried in oil is a famous dish often using roti. Often served with thick potato sambar or Nati chicken curry, it is a delicacy among the non-vegetarian communities in Siddapura.
- Banana Buns
- Ankola Koli Saaru
- Appe Huli
- Patholi
- Kalali Masala
- Thumbuli (Tambli)
- Rave Rotti

Seafood

- Chippikal Sukkha (Clams Fry)
- Kalga Sukkha
- Dry Fish chutney
- Dry Prawns chutney
- Fish barbecue
- Crab Curry

Jackfruit, banana chips, and fresh sugarcane juice are common ingredients in the area.

3

Government and Politics

GOVERNMENT OF KARNATAKA

The Government of Karnataka is a democratically elected body with the governor as the constitutional head. The governor who is appointed for five years appoints the chief minister and on the advice of the chief minister appoints his council of ministers. Even though the governor remains the ceremonial head of the state, the day-to-day running of the government is taken care of by the chief minister and his council of ministers in whom a great amount of legislative powers are vested.

Administrative divisions

Karnataka State has been divided into four revenue divisions, 49 sub-divisions, 30 districts, 176 taluks and 747 hoblies/revenue circles and 5628 gram panchayats for administrative purposes. The state has 281 towns and 7 municipal corporations. Bangalore is the fifth largest urban agglomeration out of 23 metropolis, urban agglomerations and cities in India. It is among the fastest growing cities in the world.

Political and administrative reorganisation

Karnataka took its present shape in 1956, when the states

of Mysore and Coorg (Kodagu) were merged with the Kannada-speaking districts of the former states of Bombay and Hyderabad, and Madras. Mysore state was made up of 10 districts: Bangalore, Kolar, Tumkur, Mandya, Mysore, Hassan, Chikmagalur (Kadur), Shimoga and Chitradurga; Bellary had been transferred from Madras state to Mysore in 1953, when the new Andhra State was created out of Madras' northern districts. Kodagu became a district, and Dakshina Kannada (South Kanara) district was transferred from Madras state, Uttara Kannada (North Kanara), Dharwad, Belgaum District, and Bijapur District from Bombay state, and Bidar District, Kalaburgi District, and Raichur District from Hyderabad state.

In 1989, Bangalore rural district was split from Bangalore and, in 1997, Bagalkot district split from Vijayapur, Chamrajnagar district split from Mysore, Gadag district split from Dharwad, Haveri district split from Dharwad, Koppal district split from Raichur, Udupi district split from Dakshina Kannada, and Davanagere district was created from parts of Bellary, Chitradurga, Dharwad, and Shimoga.

Legislature

The Vidhana Soudha

The state legislature is bicameral and consists of the Legislative Assembly and the Legislative Council. The Legislative Assembly consists of 224 members with one member nominated by the governor to represent the Anglo-Indian community. The term of office of the members is five years and the term of a member elected to the council is six years. The

Legislative Council is a permanent body with one-third of its members retiring every two years.

Ministry

The government is headed by the governor who appoints the chief minister and his council of ministers. The governor is appointed for five years and acts as the constitutional head of the state. Even though the governor remains the ceremonial head of the state, the day-to-day running of the government is taken care of by the chief minister and his council of ministers in whom a great deal of legislative powers is vested..

The secretariat headed by the secretary to the governor assists the council of ministers. The council of ministers consists of cabinet ministers, ministers of state and deputy ministers. The chief minister is assisted by the chief secretary, who is the head of the administrative services.

As of June 2018, the Government of Karnataka consists of 27 ministers including Chief Minister and a Deputy Chief Minister.

Chief Minister

The present Chief Minister of Karnataka is H. D. Kumaraswamy.

Karnataka Panchayat Raj

(Rule of Village Committee) is a three-tier system in the state with elected bodies at the village, taluk and district levels. It ensures greater participation of people and more effective implementation of rural development programmes. There will be a Grama Panchayat for a village or group of villages, a taluk level and the Zilla Panchayat at the district level.

All the three institutions will have elected representatives and there is no provision for nomination by the government to any of these councils. s the first in the country to enact new Panchayat Raj Act incorporating all provisions of 73rd Amendment to the Constitution. In 2014 Karantaka State Grama Panchayats Delimitation committee constituted By govt. of Karnataka. Chairmen S G Nanjaiahna mutt and 6 members.

joint secretory of the committee Dr.Revaiah Odeyar. Report Submitted 2014 October 30. This report implemented 2015 Gram Panchayath Elections.

Executive

A district of an Indian state is an administrative unit headed by a deputy commissioner or district magistrate, an officer belonging to the Indian Administrative Service. The district magistrate or the deputy commissioner is assisted by a number of officers belonging to Karnataka Civil Service and other Karnataka state services.

A Deputy Commissioner of Police, an officer belonging to the Indian Police Service is entrusted with the responsibility of maintaining law and order and related issues of the district. The commissioner is assisted by the officers of the Karnataka Police Service and other Karnataka Police officials. A Deputy Conservator of Forests, an officer belonging to the Indian Forest Service, is responsible for managing the forests, environment and wildlife related issues of the district. He is assisted by the officers of the Karnataka Forest Service and other Karnataka forest and wildlife officials. Sectoral development is looked after by the district head of each development department such as PWD, Health, Education, Agriculture, Animal husbandry, etc. These officers belong to the State Services.

Police Administration

The state is divided into 20 police districts, 77 sub-divisions, 178 circles, State Police consists of 20 police districts, 5 Police Commissioners at Bangalore, Mysore, Mangalore, belgaum and Hubli-Dharwad cities, 77 sub-divisions, 178 circles, 696 police stations, and 317 police outposts. There are six ranges: Central Range at Bangalore, Eastern Range at Davanagere, Northern Range at Gulbarga, Southern Range at Mysore and Western Range at Mangalore. The government Railway Police is headed by a D.I.G. of Police.

Units that assist the state in law and order include Criminal Investigation Department (Forest Cell, Anti-Dowry Cell, etc.), Dog Squad, Civil Rights Enforcement Wing, Police Wireless and Police Motor Transport Organization and special units. Village Defence Parties protect persons and property in the village and assist the police when necessary. The police force is at times supplemented by Home Guards.

Politics

Karnataka politics is dominated by the Bharatiya Janata party (BJP), Janata Dala Secular (JDS) and the Indian national Congress (INC).

In recent election conducted in May 2018 BJP emerged as single largest party with 104 seats leaving behind INC with 79 , JDS with 38 and others 2. While B. S. Yeddyurappa went ahead with the intention of making the government and requested the governor to allow him to form a government without the numbers though. Governor allowed him to take oath as Chief Minister on 17th May 2018 although his happiness was short lived as SC struck down 2 weeks of time provided by the governor for the floor test to just 2 days. He was forced to resign. After his resignation current Chief Minister Shri. H. D. Kumaraswamy was sworn in on 23rd May 2018 with absolute majority support from Congress total of 117.

In recent bypolls JDS+Congress combine won 4 out of 5 seats 3MP & 2 MLA seats making the numbers up by 119

Elections

Last assembly elections: Karnataka Legislative Assembly election, 2018

LNG Terminal in Karwar, Karnataka (India)

Asia's Biggest LNG Terminal in Karwar, Karnataka (India). MOU Between Fox Petroleum and Govt of Karnataka worth $1,038 Million USD has been signed between Ajay Kumar and Minister of Industry - Government of Karnataka (India Govt).

GOVERNMENT AND ADMINISTRATION

Karnataka has a parliamentary system of government with two democratically elected houses, the Legislative Assembly and the Legislative Council. The Legislative Assembly consists of 224 members who are elected for five-year terms. The Legislative Council is a permanent body of 75 members with one-third (25 members) retiring every two years.

Vidhana Soudha *in Bangalore (seat of the Legislative Assembly)*

The government of Karnataka is headed by the Chief Minister who is chosen by the ruling party members of the Legislative Assembly. The Chief Minister, along with the council of ministers, executes the legislative agenda and exercises most of the executive powers.

However, the constitutional and formal head of the state is the Governor who is appointed for a five-year term by the President of Indiaon the advice of the Union government. The people of Karnataka also elect 28 members to the *Lok Sabha*, the lower house of the Indian Parliament. The members of the state Legislative Assembly elect 12 members to the *Rajya Sabha*, the upper house of the Indian Parliament.

For administrative purposes, Karnataka has been divided into four revenue divisions, 49 sub-divisions, 30 districts, 175 *taluks* and 745 *hoblies* / revenue circles. The administration in each district is headed by a Deputy Commissioner who belongs to the Indian Administrative Service and is assisted by a number of officers belonging to Karnataka state services.

The Deputy Commissioner of Police, an officer belonging to the Indian Police Service and assisted by the officers of the Karnataka Police Service, is entrusted with the responsibility of maintaining law and order and related issues in each district. The Deputy Conservator of Forests, an officer belonging to the Indian Forest Service, is entrusted with the responsibility of managing forests, environment and wildlife of the district, he will be assisted by the officers belonging to Karnataka Forest Service and officers belonging to Karnataka Forest Subordinate Service.

Sectoral development in the districts is looked after by the district head of each development department such as Public Works Department, Health, Education, Agriculture, Animal Husbandry, etc. The judiciary in the state consists of the Karnataka High Court (*Attara Kacheri*) in Bangalore, Dharwad and Gulbarga, district and session courts in each district and lower courts and judges at the *taluk* level.

Politics in Karnataka has been dominated by three political parties, the Indian National Congress, the Janata Dal (Secular) and the Bharatiya Janata Party. Politicians from Karnataka have played prominent roles in federal government of India with some of them having held the high positions of Prime Minister and Vice-President. Border disputes involving Karnataka's claim on the Kasaragod and Solapur districts and Maharashtra's claim on Belgaum are ongoing since the states reorganisation. The official emblem of Karnataka has a *Ganda Berunda* in the centre. Surmounting this are four lions facing the four directions, taken from the Lion Capital of Ashoka at Sarnath. The emblem also carries two *Sharabhas* with the head of an elephant and the body of a lion.

KARNATAKA -HARADANAHALLI DEVEGOWDA KUMARASWAMY

Haradanahalli Devegowda Kumaraswamy is an influential Indian politician from Karnataka. He is the son of former Prime Minister, Sri. H.D. Devegowda and the leader of Janata Dal (Secular). He sworn-in as the new Chief Minister of Karnataka for the second time on 23rd May 2018. Popularly known as "Kumaranna", he has a huge fan base because of his aggressive approach.

Early life and education

Kumaraswamy was born on 16 December 1959 to H. D. Deve Gowda and Chennamma in Hassan District of Karnataka.He completed his primary schooling from a government school in Hassan District and his high school education from MES Educational Institution in Jayanagar. He completed his PUC from Vijaya College and earned his B.Sc. from the National College in Jayanagar, Bangalore.

His married life has been quite controversial. Firstly, he got married to his first wife, Anitha on 13 March, 1986, with whom he has a son named Nikhil Gowda. Then, in 2006, Kumaraswamy married Kannada actress Radhika even though his wife was still alive and they have not neen separated. He has a daughter with Radhika named Shamika K. Swamy. This marriage was seen as a violation of the marriage code under Hindu Personal Law and section 494 of Indian Penal Code. However, Karnataka High Court dismissed the case on the basis of lack of evidence.

Kumaraswamy political career

Kumaraswamy made his entry into politics after winning the general elections in 1996 from Kanakapura Lok Sabha constituency. Just like his father, he too enjoys the support of the powerful Vokkaligga community in the state.

The state of Karnataka faced the similar situation as in 2018 of a fractured mandate in 2004. At that time, the Congress and JD(S) had joined their hands and formed a coalition government. Dharam Singh of the Congress, being the unanimous choice of both parties, was elected to head the government and was sworn-in as the Chief Minister of Karnataka on 28 May 2004.

Kumaraswamy, along with 42 MLAs of the Janata Dal (Secular), left the coalition on January 28, 2006, after which the government collapsed. Later on, when Karnataka Governor T. N. Chaturvedi reached out to Kumaraswamy to form the government in the state, Kumaraswamy became the chief minister of Karnataka from 4 February 2006 to 9 October 2007 under a power-sharing agreement with the BJP.

He resigned from his chief ministerial post after denying transferring the power to BJP as per the agreement.

Kumaraswamy was elected as Karnataka state Janata Dal (Secular) President in November 2014.

In 2018 elections in Karnataka state, JD(S) was on the third position with just 36 seats in its kitty but after a post-poll alliance with the Indian National Congress, he became the Chief Minister on 23rd May 2018.

His Achievements

Kumaraswamy's contributions in taking his state to the next level are something to be admired and appreciated. He has made a mark for himself through people-friendly programmes, which benefited both rural and urban masses. He relentlessly supported the industries and was also committed to improving infrastructural facilities in Karnataka.

He focused on the upgradation of the areas located on the outskirts of Bangalore by taking up several developmental projects.

While taking a tour around the nooks and corners of the state, he interacted with the people, noted their problems, and directed his officials to help them in every possible way. In Bangalore, he started a weekly initiative, Janatha Darshana, which was the biggest popular programme in the state.

GOVERNORS OF KARNATAKA

The Governor of Karnataka is the constitutional head of each of the south Indian state of Karnataka. The governor is appointed by the President of India for a term of five years, and holds office at the President's pleasure.

The governor is *de jure* head of the Government of Karnataka; all its executive actions are taken in the governor's name. However, the governor must act on the advice of the popularly elected council of ministers, headed by the Chief Minister of Karnataka, which thus holds *de facto* executive authority in the state.

The Constitution of India also empowers the governor to act upon his or her own discretion, such as the ability to appoint or dismiss a ministry, recommend President's rule, or reserve bills for the President's assent. Over the years, the exercise of these discretionary powers have given rise to conflict between the elected chief minister and the central government–appointed governor.

Since 1956, eighteen people have served as the Governor of

Mysore (as the state was known before 1 November 1973) and Karnataka. The first was Jayachamarajendra Wadiyar, previously the Maharaja of Mysore (1940–50) and the Rajpramukh of Mysore (1950–56). A majority of Karnataka's governors have been politicians (ten), another five have been civil servants. V. V. Giri went on become the fourth President of India, and Gopal Swarup Pathak the country's fourth Vice President.

4

Language and Literature

LANGUAGE

Distribution of languages in Karnataka

Kannada (66.54%)

Urdu (10.83%)

Telugu (5.84%)

Tamil (3.45%)

Marathi (3.38%)

Hindi (3.30%)

Tulu (2.61%)

Others (4.05%)

The Kannada language serves as the official language of the state of Karnataka, as the native language of approximately 65% of its population and as one of the classical languages of India. Kannada played a crucial role in the creation of Karnataka: linguistic demographics played a major role in defining the new state in 1956. Tulu, Konkani and Kodava are other minor native languages that share a long history in the state. Urdu is spoken widely by the Muslim population. Less widely spoken languages include Beary bashe and certain languages such as Sankethi. Some of the regional languages in Karnataka are Tulu, Kodava, Konkani and Beary.

Kannada features a rich and ancient body of literature including religious and secular genre, covering topics as diverse as Jainism (such as *Puranas*), Veerashaivism (such as Vachanas), Vaishnavism (such as *Haridasa Sahitya*) and modern literature. Evidence from edicts during the time of Ashoka (reigned 274–232 BCE) suggest that Buddhist literature influenced the Kannada script and its literature. The Halmidi inscription, the earliest attested full-length inscription in the Kannada language and script, dates from 450 CE, while the earliest available literary work, the *Kavirajamarga*, has been dated to 850 CE. References made in the *Kavirajamarga*, however, prove that Kannada literature flourished in the native composition meters such as *Chattana*, *Beddande* and *Melvadu* during earlier centuries. The classic refers to several earlier greats (*purvacharyar*) of Kannada poetry and prose.

Halmidi inscription (450 CE) is the earliest attested inscription in the Kannada language.

Kuvempu, the renowned Kannada poet and writer who wrote Jaya Bharata Jananiya Tanujate, the state anthem of Karnataka was the first recipient of the "Karnataka Ratna" award, the highest civilian award bestowed by the Government of Karnataka. Contemporary Kannada literature has received considerable acknowledgement in the arena of Indian literature, with eight Kannada writers winning India's highest literary honour, the Jnanpith award.

Tulu is spoken mainly in the coastal districts of Udupi and Dakshina Kannada. *Tulu Mahabharato*, written by Arunabja in the Tigalari script, is the oldest surviving Tulu text.Tigalari script was used by Brahmins to write Sanskrit language. The use of the Kannada script for writing Tulu and non-availability of print in Tigalari script contributed to the marginalisation of Tigalari script. Konkani is mostly spoken in the Uttara Kannada and Dakshina Kannada districts and in parts of Udupi, Konkani use the Kannada script for writing. The Kodavas who mainly reside in the Kodagu district, speak Kodava Takk. Two regional variations of the language exist, the northern *Mendale Takka* and the southern *Kiggaati Takka*. Kodava Takk use the Kannada script for writing. English is the medium of education in many schools and widely used for business communication in most private companies.

All of the state's languages are patronised and promoted by governmental and quasi-governmental bodies. The *Kannada Sahitya Parishat* and the *Kannada Sahitya Akademi* are responsible for the promotion of Kannada while the *Karnataka Konkani Sahitya Akademi*, the *Tulu Sahitya Akademi* and the *Kodava Sahitya Akademi* promote their respective languages.

KANNADA LANGUAGE

Kannada is a Dravidian language spoken predominantly by Kannada people in India, mainly in the state of Karnataka, and by significant linguistic minorities in the states of Andhra Pradesh, Telangana, Tamil Nadu, Kerala and abroad. The language has roughly 43.7 million native speakers, who are called Kannadigas (*Kannadigaru*). Kannada is also spoken as a second and third language by over 12.9 million non-Kannada speakers living in Karnataka, which adds up to 56.6 million speakers. It is one of the scheduled languages of India and the official and administrative language of the state of Karnataka.

The Kannada language is written using the Kannada script, which evolved from the 5th-century Kadamba script. Kannada is attested epigraphically for about one and a half millennia, and literary Old Kannada flourished in the 6th-century Ganga dynasty and during the 9th-century Rashtrakuta Dynasty. Kannada has an unbroken literary history of over a thousand years. Kannada literature has been presented with 8 Jnanapeeth awards, the most for any Dravidian language and the second highest for any Indian language.

Based on the recommendations of the Committee of Linguistic Experts, appointed by the ministry of culture, the government of Indiadesignated Kannada a classical language of India. Kannada is considered to be one of the oldest living languages . In July 2011, a centre for the study of classical Kannada was established as part of the Central Institute of Indian Languages at Mysore to facilitate research related to the language.

Development

Kannada is a Southern Dravidian language, and according to Dravidian scholar Sanford B. Steever, its history can be conventionally divided into three periods: Old Kannada (*Halegannada*) from 450–1200 CE, Middle Kannada (*Nadugannada*) from 1200–1700, and Modern Kannada from 1700 to the present. Kannada is influenced to an appreciable extent by Sanskrit. Influences of other languages such as Prakrit and Pali can also be found in the Kannada language. The scholar Iravatham Mahadevan indicated that Kannada was already a language of rich oral tradition earlier than the 3rd century BCE, and based on the native Kannada words found in Prakrit inscriptions of that period, Kannada must have been spoken by a widespread and stable population. The scholar K. V. Narayana claims that many tribal languages which are now designated as Kannada dialects could be nearer to the earlier form of the language, with lesser influence from other languages.

Sanskrit and Prakrit influence

The sources of influence on literary Kannada grammar appear to be three-fold: Pânini's grammar, non-Paninian schools of Sanskritgrammar, particularly *Katantra* and *Sakatayana* schools, and Prakrit grammar. Literary Prakrit seems to have prevailed in Karnataka since ancient times. The vernacular Prakrit speaking people may have come into contact with Kannada speakers, thus influencing their language, even before Kannada was used for administrative or liturgical purposes. Kannada phonetics, morphology, vocabulary, grammar and syntax show significant influence from these languages.

History

Early traces

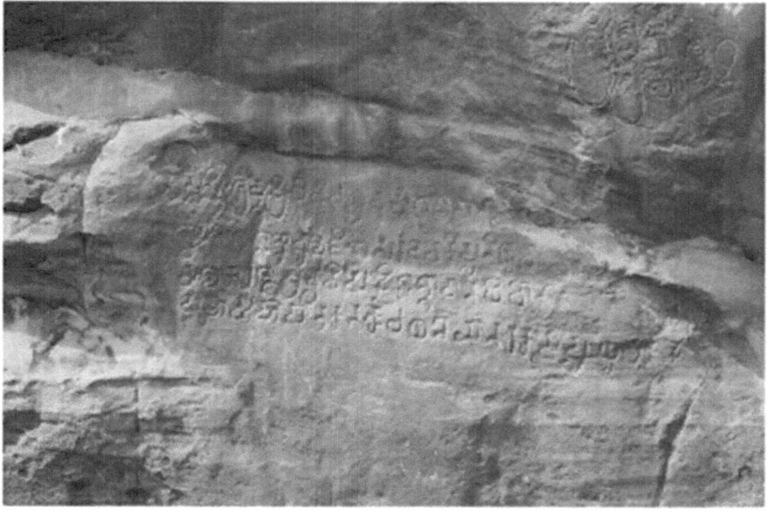

Purava HaleGannada: This Kannada term literally translated means "Previous form of Old Kannada" was the language of Banavasi in the early Common Era, the Satavahana, Chutu Satakarni (Naga) and Kadambaperiods and thus has a history of over 2500 years. The Ashoka rock edict found at Brahmagiri (dated to 230 BCE) has been suggested to contain words in identifiable Kannada. According to Jain tradition,

Brahmi, the daughter of Rishabhadeva, the first Tirthankara of Jainism, invented 18 alphabets, including Kannada, which points to the antiquity of the language. Supporting this tradition, an inscription of about the 9th century CE, containing specimens of different alphabets, mostly Dravidian, was discovered in a Jain temple in the Deogarh fort.

Greek dramatists Euripides (480-406 BCE) and Aristophanes (446-386 BCE) of the 5th–4th century BCE were purportedly familiar with the Kannada country and language which can be concluded by the usage of Kannada words, phrases and expressions in their Greek plays along with Persian and Punic. This would show a far more intimate contact of the Greeks with Kannada culture than with Indian culture elsewhere.

The Kannada word *Ooralli* (*lit* it means "in a village") is said to be written on a huge wall constructed in Alexandria in the 4th century BCE as part of the remnants of 36,000 palm manuscripts that had been burnt in an accidental fire in Alexander's time. The palm manuscripts contained texts written not only in Greek, Latin and Hebrew, but also in Sanskrit and Kannada.

In some 3rd–1st century BCE Tamil inscriptions, words of Kannada influence such as '*nalliyooraa*', '*kavuDi*' and '*posil*' have been introduced. The use of the vowel '*a*' as an adjective is not prevalent in Tamil but its usage is available in Kannada. Kannada words such as '*gouDi-gavuDi*' transform into Tamil's '*kavuDi*' for lack of the usage of *Ghosha svana* in Tamil. Hence the Kannada word 'gavuDi' becomes 'kavuDi' in Tamil. 'Posil' ('hosilu') was introduced into Tamil from Kannada and colloquial Tamil uses this word as 'Vaayil'. In a 1st-century CE Tamil inscription, there is a personal reference to '*ayjayya*', a word of Kannada origin. In a 3rd-century CE Tamil inscription there is usage of '*oppanappa vIran*'. Here the honorific '*appa*' to a person's name is an influence from Kannada. Another word of Kannada origin is '*taayviru*' and is found in a 4th-century CE Tamil inscription. S. Settar studied the '*sittanvAsal*' inscription of first century CE as also the inscriptions at '*tirupparamkunram*', '*adakala*' and '*neDanUpatti*'. The later inscriptions were studied in detail by Iravatham Mahadevan also. Mahadevan argues that the words '*erumi*', '*kavuDi*', '*poshil*' and '*tAyiyar*' have their origin in Kannada because Tamil cognates are not available. Settar adds the words '*nADu*' and '*iLayar*' to this list. Mahadevan feels that some grammatical categories found in these inscriptions are also unique to Kannada rather than Tamil. Both these scholars attribute these influences to the movements and spread of Jainas in these regions. These inscriptions belong to the period between the first century BCE and fourth century CE. These are some examples that are proof of the influence of Kannada on Tamil before the common era and in the early centuries of the common era.

In the 150 CE Prakrit book *Gaathaa Saptashati*, written by Haala Raja, Kannada words like *tIr or Teer (*meaning *to be able), tuppa, peTTu, poTTu, poTTa, piTTu (*meaning *to strike), Pode (Hode)* have been used. On the Pallava Prakrit inscription of 250 CE of Hire Hadagali's Shivaskandavarman, the Kannada word *kOTe* transforms into *koTTa*. In the 350 CE Chandravalli Prakrit inscription, words of Kannada origin like *punaaTa, puNaDa* have been used. In one more Prakrit inscription of 250 CE found in Malavalli, Kannada towns like *vEgooraM* (*bEgooru*), *kundamuchchaMDi* find a reference.

Pliny the Elder (23 – 79 CE) was a naval and army commander in the early Roman Empire. He writes about pirates between Muziris and Nitrias (Netravati River). He also mentions Barace (Barcelore). Nitrias of Pliny and Nitran of Ptolemy refer to the Netravati River as also the modern port city of Mangaluru, upon its mouth. Many of these are Kannada origin names of places and rivers of the Karnataka coast of 1st century CE.

The Greek geographer Ptolemy (150 CE) mentions places such as Badiamaioi (Badami), Inde (Indi), Kalligeris (Kalkeri), Modogoulla (Mudagal), Petrigala (Pattadakal), Hippokoura (Huvina Hipparagi), Nagarouris (Nagur), Tabaso (Tavasi), Tiripangalida (Gadahinglai), Soubouttou or Sabatha (Savadi), Banaouase (Banavasi), Thogorum (Tagara), Biathana (Paithan), Sirimalaga (Malkhed), Aloe (Ellapur) and Pasage (Palasige) indicating prosperous trade between Egypt, Europe and Karnataka. He also mentions Pounnata (Punnata) and refers to beryls, i.e., the *Vaidhurya* gems of that country. He mentions Malippala (Malpe) a coastal town of Karnataka. In this work Larika and Kandaloi are identified as Rastrika and Kuntala. Ptolemy writes in the midst of the false mouth and the Barios, there is a city called Maganur (Mangalore). He mentions of inland centres of pirates called Oloikhora (Alavakheda). He mentions Ariake Sadinon meaning Aryaka Satakarni and Baithana as capital of Siro(e) P(t)olmaios, i.e., Sri Pulimayi clearly indicating his knowledge of the Satavahana kings. The word *Pulimayi* means *One with body of Tiger* in Kannada, which bears testimony to the possible Kannada origin of Satavahana kings.

A possibly more definite reference to Kannada is found in the 'Charition Mime' ascribed to the late 1st to early 2nd century CE. The farce, written by an unknown author, is concerned with a Greek lady named Charition who has been stranded on the coast of a country bordering the Indian Ocean. The king of this region, and his countrymen, sometimes use their own language, and the sentences they speak could be interpreted as Kannada, including *Koncha madhu patrakke haki* ("Having poured a little wine into the cup separately") and *paanam beretti katti madhuvam ber ettuvenu* ("Having taken up the cup separately and having covered it, I shall take wine separately."). The language employed in the papyrus indicates that the play is set in one of the numerous small ports on the western coast of India, between Karwar and Kanhangad (presently in Kerala). The character of the king in this farce refers to himself as 'the Nayaka of Malpe (Malpi-naik)'. B. A. Saletore identifies the site of this play as Odabhandeshwara or Vadabhandeshwara (ship-vessel-Ishwara or God), situated about a mile from Malpe, which was a Shaivite centre originally surrounded by a forest with a small river passing through it. He rejects M. Govinda Pai's opinion that it must have occurred at Udyavara (Odora in Greek), the capital of Alupas. Stavros J. Tsitsiridis mentions in his research work that *Charition* is not an exclusively prose or verse text, but a mixed form. The corrupt lines indicate that the text found at Oxyrhynchus (Egypt) has been copied, meaning that the original was even earlier in date. Wilamowitz (1907) and Andreassi (2001) say that for more precise dating of the original, some place the composition of the work as early as in the Hellenistic period (332-30 BCE), others at a later date, up to the early 2nd c. CE.

Epigraphy

The earliest examples of a full-length Kannada language stone inscription (*shilaashaasana*) containing Brahmi characters with characteristics attributed to those of proto-Kannada in *Hale Kannada* (*lit* Old Kannada) script can be found in the Halmidi inscription, usually dated c. AD 450, indicating that Kannada had become an administrative language at that time. The Halmidi inscription provides invaluable information about the history and culture of Karnataka. The Kannada inscription excavated at the Pranaveshwara temple complex at Talagunda near Shiralakoppa in Shikaripur taluk of Shivamogga district, dated to 370 CE is said to be one of the earliest Kannada inscriptions replacing the Halmidi inscription of 450 CE. The 5th century Tamatekallu inscription of Chitradurga and the Chikkamagaluruinscription of 500 AD are further examples. Recent reports indicate that the Old Kannada *Nishadi*inscription discovered on the Chandragiri hill, Shravanabelagola, is older than Halmidi inscription by about fifty to hundred years and may belong to the period AD 350–400. The noted archaeologist and art historian S. Shettar is of the opinion that an inscription of the Western Ganga King Kongunivarma Madhava (c. 350–370) found at Tagarthi (Tyagarthi) in Shikaripura taluk of Shimoga district is of 350 CE and is also older than the Halmidi inscription.

Current estimates of the total number of existing epigraphs written in Kannada range from 25,000 by the scholar Sheldon Pollock to over 30,000 by the Amaresh Datta of the Sahitya Akademi. Prior to the Halmidi inscription, there is an abundance of inscriptions containing Kannada words, phrases and sentences, proving its antiquity. The 543 AD Badami cliff inscription of Pulakesi I is an example of a Sanskrit inscription in old Kannada script. Kannada inscriptions are not only discovered in Karnataka but also quite commonly in Andhra

Pradesh and Telangana, Maharashtra and Tamil Nadu. Some inscriptions were also found in Madhya Pradesh and Gujarat. The Northern most Kannada inscription of the Rashtrakutas of 964 CE is the Jura record found near Jabalpur in present-day Madhya Pradesh, belonging to the reign of Krishna III. This indicates the spread of the influence of the language over the ages, especially during the rule of large Kannada empires. Pyu sites of Myanmar yielded variety of Indian scripts including those written in a script especially archaic, most resembling the Kadamba (Kannada-speaking Kadambas of 4th century CE Karnataka and Andhra Pradesh) form of common Kannada-Telugu script from Andhra Pradesh.

The earliest copper plates inscribed in Old Kannada script and language, dated to the early 8th century AD, are associated with Alupa King Aluvarasa II from Belmannu (the Dakshina Kannada district), and display the double crested fish, his royal emblem. The oldest well-preserved palm leaf manuscript in *Old Kannada* is that of *Dhavala*. It dates to around the 9th century and is preserved in the Jain Bhandar, Mudbidri, Dakshina Kannada district. The manuscript contains 1478 leaves written using ink.

Coins

Some early Kadamba Dynasty coins bearing the Kannada inscription *Vira* and *Skandha* were found in Satara collectorate. A gold coin bearing three inscriptions of *Sri* and an abbreviated inscription of king Bhagiratha's name called *bhagi* (c. AD 390–420) in old Kannada exists. A Kadamba copper coin dated to the 5th century AD with the inscription *Srimanaragi* in Kannada script was discovered in Banavasi, Uttara Kannada district.Coins with Kannada legends have been discovered spanning the rule of the Western Ganga Dynasty, the Badami Chalukyas, the Alupas, the Western Chalukyas, the Rashtrakutas, the Hoysalas, the Vijayanagar Empire, the Kadamba Dynasty of Banavasi, the Keladi Nayakas and the Mysore Kingdom, the Badami Chalukya coins being a recent discovery. The coins of the Kadambas of Goa are unique in that they have alternate inscription of the king's name in Kannada and Devanagari in triplicate, a few coins of the Kadambas of Hangal are also available.

KANNADA LITERATURE

Kannada literature is the corpus of written forms of the Kannada language, a member of the Dravidian family spoken mainly in the Indian state of Karnataka and written in the Kannada script.

Attestations in literature span something like one and a half millennia, with some specific literary works surviving in rich manuscript traditions, extending from the 9th century to the present. The Kannada language is usually divided into three linguistic phases: Old (450–1200 CE), Middle (1200–1700 CE) and Modern (1700–present); and its literary characteristics are categorised as Jain, Veerashaiva and Vaishnava—recognising the prominence of these three faiths in giving form to, and fostering, classical expression of the language, until the advent of the modern era. Although much of the literature prior to the 18th century was religious, some secular works were also committed to writing.

Starting with the *Kavirajamarga* (*c*. 850), and until the middle of the 12th century, literature in Kannada was almost exclusively composed by the Jains, who found eager patrons in the Chalukya, Ganga, Rashtrakuta, Hoysala and the Yadava kings.Although the *Kavirajamarga*, authored during the reign of King Amoghavarsha, is the oldest extant literary work in the language, it has been generally accepted by modern scholars that prose, verse and grammatical traditions must have existed earlier.

The Veerashaiva movement of the 12th century created new literature which flourished alongside the Jain works. With the waning of Jain influence during the 14th-century Vijayanagara empire, a new Vaishnava literature grew rapidly in the 15th century; the devotional movement of the itinerant Haridasa saints marked the high point of this era.

After the decline of the Vijayanagara empire in the 16th century, Kannada literature was supported by the various rulers, including the Wodeyars of the Kingdom of Mysore and the

Nayakas of Keladi. In the 19th century, some literary forms, such as the prose narrative, the novel, and the short story, were borrowed from English literature. Modern Kannada literature is now widely known and recognised: during the last half century, Kannada language authors have received eight Jnanpith awards, 60 Sahitya Akademi awards and 9 Sahitya Akademi Fellowships in India.

Content and genre

In the early period and beginning of the medieval period, between the 9th and 13th centuries, writers were predominantly Jains and Lingayats. Jains were the earliest known cultivators of Kannada literature, which they dominated until the 12th century, although a few works by Lingayats from that period have survived. Jain authors wrote about Tirthankaras and other aspects of religion. The Veerashaiva authors wrote about Shiva, his 25 forms, and the expositions of Shaivism. Lingayat poets belonging to the vachana sahitya tradition advanced the philosophy of Basava from the 12th century.

During the period between the 13th and 15th centuries, there was decline in Jain writings and an increase in the number of works from the Lingayat tradition; there were also contributions from Vaishnava writers. Thereafter, Lingayat and Vaishnava writers dominated Kannada literature. Vaishnava writers focused on the Hindu epics – the Ramayana, the Mahabharata and the Bhagavata – as well as Vedanta and other subjects from the Puranic traditions. The devotional songs of the Haridasa poets, performed to music, were first noted in the 15th century. Writings on secular subjects remained popular throughout this period.

An important change during the Bhakti "devotion" period starting in the 12th century was the decline of court literature and the rise in popularity of shorter genres such as the *vachana* and *kirthane*, forms that were more accessible to the common man. Writings eulogising kings, commanders and spiritual heroes waned, with a proportional increase in the use of local genres. Kannada literature moved closer to the spoken and sung folk traditions, with musicality being its hallmark, although some poets continued to use the ancient *champu* form of writing as late as the 17th century.

Kannada poetry on stone–7th century Kappe Arabhattainscription

The *champu* Sanskritic metre (poems in verses of various metres interspersed with paragraphs of prose, also known as *champu-kavya*) was the most popular written form from the 9th century onwards, although it started to fall into disuse in the 12th century. Other Sanskritic metres used were the *saptapadi* (seven line verse), the *ashtaka* (eight line verse) and the *shataka* (hundred-line verse). There were numerous translations and adaptations of Sanskrit writings into Kannada and, to a lesser extent, from Kannada into Sanskrit. The medieval period saw the development of literary metres indigenous to the Kannada language. These included the *tripadi* (three-line verse, in use from the 7th century), one of the oldest native metres; the *shatpadi* (six-line verse, first mentioned by Nagavarma I in *Chhandombudhi* of c. 984 and in use from 1165), of which six types exist; the *ragale*(lyrical narrative compositions, in use from 1160); the *sangatya* (compositions meant to be sung with a musical instrument, in use from 1232) and the *akkara* which came to be adopted in some Teluguwritings. There were rare interactions with Tamil literature, as well.

Though religious literature was prominent, literary genres including romance, fiction, erotica, satire, folk songs, fables and parables, musical treatises and musical compositions were popular. The topics of Kannada literature included grammar, philosophy, prosody, rhetoric, chronicles, biography, history, drama and cuisine, as well as dictionaries and encyclopedias. According to critic Joseph T. Shipley, over fifty works on scientific subjects including medicine, mathematics and astrology have been written in the Kannada language.

Kannada literature of this period was mainly written on palm leaves. However, more than 30,000 more durable inscriptions on stone (known as *shilashasana*) and copper plates (known as *tamrashasana*) have survived to inform modern students of the historical development of Kannada literature. The Shravanabelagola inscription of Nandisena (7th century), Kappe Arabhatta inscription (c. 700), and the Hummacha and Soraba inscriptions (c. 800) are good examples of poetry in *tripadi* metre, and the Jura (Jabalpur) inscription of King Krishna III (964) is regarded as an epigraphical landmark of classical Kannada composition, containing poetic diction in *kanda* metre, a form consisting of a group of stanzas or chapters.

Elegiac poetry on hundreds of *veeragallu* and *maastigallu* (hero stones) written by unknown poets in the *kanda* and the *vritta* (commentary) metre mourn the death of heroes who sacrificed their lives and the bravery of women who performed *sati*. According to the scholar T. V. Venkatachala Sastry, the book *Karnataka Kavicharitre* compiled by Kannada scholar R. Narasimhachar lists over one thousand anonymous pieces of

Kannada literature that cover an array of topics under religious and secular categories. Some fifty *Vachana*poets are known only by the pen names (*ankita*) used in their poems. Most Jain writings included in the list are from the period 1200–1450 CE, while Veerashaiva and Vaishnava writings are from later periods. Secular topics include mathematics, medicine, science of horses and elephants, architecture, geography and hydrology.

The pace of change towards more modern literary styles gained momentum in the early 19th century. Kannada writers were initially influenced by the modern literature of other languages, especially English. Modern English education and liberal democratic values inspired social changes, intertwined with the desire to retain the best of traditional ways.New genres including short stories, novels, literary criticism, and essays, were embraced as Kannada prose moved toward modernisation.

Hoysala period

In the late 12th century, the Hoysalas, a powerful hill tribe from the Malnad region in modern southern Karnataka, exploited the political uncertainty in the Deccan to gain dominance in the region south of the Krishna River in southern India. A new chronological era was adopted, imperial titles were claimed and Kannada literature flourished with such noted scholars as Janna, Harihara, Rudrabhatta, Raghavanka, Keshiraja and others. An important achievement during this period was the establishment of native metres in literature (the *ragale*, the *tripadi*, the *sangatya* and the *shatpadi*).

Two renowned philosophers who lived during this time, Ramanujacharya and Madhvacharya, influenced the culture of the region. The conversion of the Hoysala King Vishnuvardhana in the early 12th century from Jainism to Vaishnavism was to later prove a setback to Jain literature. In the decades to follow, Jain writers faced competition from the Veerashaivas, to which they responded with rebuttals, and from the 15th century, from the writers of the Vaishnava cadre. These events changed the literary landscape of the Kannada-speaking region forever.

Hero stone **(virgal)** *with* **old Kannada** *elegiac inscription (1220) at the Ishwara temple in Arasikere, Karnataka*

One of the earliest Veerashaiva writers who was not part of the *Vachana* literary tradition, poet Harihara (or Harisvara) came from a family of *karnikas*(accountants), and worked under the patronage of King Narasimha I. He wrote *Girijakalyana* in ten sections following the Kalidasa tradition, employing the old Jain *champu* style, with the story leading to the marriage of Shiva and Parvati. In a deviation from the norm, Harihara avoided glorifying saintly mortals. He is credited with more than 100 poems in *ragale* metre, called the *Nambiyanana ragale* (or *Shivaganada ragale*, 1160) praising the saint Nambiyana and Virupaksha (a form of Hindu god Shiva). For his poetic talent, he has earned the honorific *utsava kavi*("poet of exuberance").

Harihara's nephew, Raghavanka, was the first to introduce the *shatpadi* metre into Kannada literature in his epic

Harishchandra Kavya (1200), considered a classic despite occasionally violating strict rules of Kannada grammar. Drawing on his skill as a dramatist, Raghavanka's story of King Harishchandra vividly describes the clash of personalities between sage Vishvamitra and sage Vashisht and between Harishchandra and Vishvamitra. It is believed that this interpretation of the story of Harishchandra is unique to Indian literature. The writing is an original and does not follow any established epic traditions. In addition to Hoysala patronage, Raghavanka was honoured by Kakatiya king Prataparudra I.

Rudrabhatta, a Smartha Brahmin (believer of monistic philosophy), was the earliest well-known Brahminical writer, under the patronage of Chandramouli, a minister of King Veera Ballala II. Based on the earlier work of *Vishnu Purana*, he wrote *Jagannatha Vijaya* (1180) in the *champu* style, relating the life of Lord Krishna leading up to his fight with the demon Banasura.

In 1209, the Jain scholar and army commander Janna wrote *Yashodhara Charite*, a unique set of stories dealing with perversion. In one of the stories, a king intended to perform a ritual sacrifice of two young boys to Mariamma, a local deity. After hearing the boys' tale, the king is moved to release them and renounce the practice of human sacrifice. In honour of this work, Janna received the title *Kavichakravarthi* ("Emperor among poets") from King Veera Ballala II. His other classic, *Anathanatha Purana* (1230), deals with the life of the 14th Tirthankar Ananthanatha.

Vijayanagara period

The 14th century saw major upheavals in geo-politics of southern India with Muslim empires invading from the north. The Vijayanagara Empire stood as a bulwark against these invasions and created an atmosphere conducive to the development of the fine arts. In a golden age of Kannada literature, competition between Vaishnava and Veerashaiva writers was fierce and literary disputations between the two sects were common, especially in the court of King Deva Raya II. Acute rivalry led to "organised processions" in honour of the classics written by poets of the respective sects. The king himself was no less a writer, the romantic stories *Sobagina Sone* (*lit* "The Drizzle of Beauty") and *Amaruka* are assigned to him.

King Krishnadevaraya, patron of Vaishnava literature

To this period belonged Kumara Vyasa (the pen name of Naranappa), a doyen of medieval epic poets and one of the most influential Vaishnava poets of the time. He was particularly known for his sophisticated use of metaphors and had even earned the title *Rupaka Samrajya Chakravarti*("Emperor of the land of Metaphors"). In 1430, he wrote the *Gadugina Bharata*, popularly known as *Karnata Bharata Kathamanjari* or *Kumaravyasa Bharata* in the Vyasa tradition. The work is a translation of the first ten chapters of the epic *Mahabharata* and emphasises the divinity and grace of the Lord Krishna, portraying all characters with the exception of Krishna to suffer from human foibles. An interesting aspect of the work is the sense of humour exhibited by the poet and his hero, Krishna. This work marked a transition of Kannada literature to a more modern genre and heralded a new age combining poetic perfection with religious inspiration. The remaining *parvas* (chapters) of *Mahabharata* were translated by Timmanna Kavi (1510) in the court of King Krishnadevaraya. The poet named his work *Krishnaraya Bharata* after his patron king.

Kumara Valmiki (1500) wrote the first complete brahminical adaptation of the epic Ramayana, called *Torave Ramayana*. According to the author, the epic he wrote merely narrated God Shiva's conversation with his consort Parvati. This writing has remained popular for centuries and inspired folk theatre such as the *Yakshagana*, which has made use of its verses as a script for enacting episodes from the great epic. In Valmiki's version of the epic, King Ravana is depicted as one of the suitors at Sita's *Swayamvara* (*lit.* a ceremony of "choice of a husband"). His failure to win the bride's hand results in jealousy towards Rama, the eventual bridegroom. As the story progresses, Hanuman, for all his services to Rama, is exalted to the status of "the next creator". Towards the end of the story, during the war with Rama, Ravana realises that his adversary is none other than the God Vishnu and hastens to die at his hands to achieve salvation.

Chamarasa, a Veerashaiva poet, was a rival of Kumara Vyasa in the court of Devaraya II. His eulogy of the saint Allama Prabhu, titled *Prabhulinga Lile* (1430), was later translated into Telugu and Tamil at the behest of his patron king. In the story, the saint was considered an incarnation of Hindu God Ganapathi while Parvati took the form of a princess of Banavasi.

Interaction between Kannada and Telugu literatures, a trend which had begun in the Hoysala period, increased. Translations of classics from Kannada to Telugu and vice versa became popular. Well-known bilingual poets of this period were Bhima Kavi, Piduparti Somanatha and Nilakanthacharya. In fact, so well versed in Kannada were some Telugu poets, including Dhurjati, that they freely used many Kannada terms in their Telugu writings. It was because of this "familiarity" with Kannada, that the notable writer Srinatha even called his Telugu, "Kannada". This process of interaction between the two languages continued into the 19th century in the form of translations by bilingual writers.

TULU LANGUAGE

Tulu is a Dravidian language spoken mainly in the south west part of the Indian state of Karnataka and also in the Kasaragod district of Kerala. The Tulu speaking region is often referred to as Tulu Nadu. The native speakers of Tulu are referred to as *Tuluva* or Tulu people.

The Indian census report of 2011 reported a total of 1,846,427 native Tulu speakers in India. The 2001 census had reported a total of 1,722,768 native speakers, According to one estimate reported in 2009, Tulu is currently spoken by 3 to 5 million speakers in the world. There is some difficulty in counting Tulu speakers who have migrated from their native region as they often get counted as Kannada speakers in Indian Census reports

Separated early from Proto-South Dravidian, Tulu has several features not found in Tamil–Kannada. For example, it has the pluperfect and the future perfect, like French or Spanish, but formed without an auxiliary verb.

Robert Caldwell, in his pioneering work *A Comparative Grammar of the Dravidian or South-Indian family of languages*, called this language "peculiar and very interesting". According to him, "Tulu is one of the most highly developed languages of the Dravidian family. It looks as if it had been cultivated for its own sake."

Tulu is the primary spoken language in Tulu Nadu, a region comprising the districts of Dakshina Kannada and Udupi in the west of the state of Karnataka and the Kasaragod taluk. Non-native speakers of Tulu include those who speak the Beary language, Havyakaand Gowda dialects of Kannada as also Konkani, Koraga and Malayalam speakers resident in the Tulu Nadu region. Apart from Tulu Nadu, a significant emigrant population of Tulu speaking people is found in Maharashtra,

Bangalore, Chennai, the English-speaking world, and the Gulf countries.

The various medieval inscriptions of Tulu from the 15th century are in the Tigalari or Tulu script. Two Tulu epics named *Sri Bhagavato*and *Kaveri* from the 17th century were also written in the same script. However, in modern times the Tulu language is mostly written using the Kannada script. The Tulu language is known for its oral literature in the form of epic poems called *Paddana* .The Epic of Siriand the legend of Koti and Chennayya belong to this category of Tulu literature.

Classification

Tulu belongs to the southern branch of the family of Dravidian languages. It descends directly from Proto-Southern Dravidian, which in turn descends directly from Proto-Dravidian, the hypothesised mother language from which all Dravidian languages descend. The Tulu language originates in the southern part of India.

Etymology

Linguists Purushottama Bilimale have suggested that the word "Tulu" means "that which is connected with water", based on words from Kannada and Tamil. "Tulave" (jack fruit) means "watery" in Tulu; and, other water-related words in Tulu include "talipu", "teli", "teLi", "teLpu", "tuLipu", "tulavu", and "tamel". In Kannada, there are words such as tuLuku means "that which has characteristics of water" and toLe In Tamil, thuli means drop of water; and, thulli means the same in Malayalam.

Official status

Tulu is not currently an official language of India or any other country. Efforts are being made to include Tulu to the 8th Schedule of the Constitution. In August 2017, an online campaign was organized to include Tulu to 8th schedule of constitution and in October 2017, when the prime minister, Narendra Modi visited Dharmasthala Temple same demand was presented in front of him.

History

The oldest available inscriptions in Tulu are from the period between 14th to 15th century AD. These inscriptions are in the Tigalari script and are found in areas in and around Barkur which was the capital of Tulu Nadu during the Vijayanagar period. Another group of inscriptions are found in the *Ullur Subrahmanya* Temple near Kundapura. Many linguists like S.U. Panniyadi and L. V. Ramaswami Iyer as well as P.S. Subrahmanya suggested that Tulu is among the oldest languages in the Dravidian family which branched independently from its Proto-Dravidian roots nearly 500 years ago. This assertion is based on the fact that Tulu still preserves many aspects of the Proto-Dravidian language.

This dating of Tulu is also based on the fact that the region where Tulu is natively spoken was known to the ancient Tamils as Tulu Nadu. Also, the Tamil poet Mamular who belongs to the Sangam Age (200 AD) describes Tulu Nadu and its dancing beauties in one of his poems. In the Halmidi inscriptions one finds mention of the Tulu country as the kingdom of the Alupas. The region was also known to the Greeks of the 2nd century as *Tolokoyra*. The history of Tulu would not be complete without the mention of the Charition mime, a Greek play belonging to 2nd century BC. The play's plot centres around the coastal Karnataka, where Tulu is mainly spoken. The play is mostly in Greek, but the Indian characters in the play are seen speaking a language different from Greek.

There is considerable ambiguity regarding the Indian language in the play, though all scholars agree the Indian language is Dravidian, but there is considerable dispute over which one. Noted German Indologist Dr. E. Hultzsch was the first to suggest that the language was Dravidian. The dispute regarding the language in the play is yet to be settled, but scholars agree that the dispute arises from the fact that Old Kannada, Old Tamil and Tulu during the time when the play was written were perhaps dialectical variations of the same proto-language, and that over the years they evolved into their present forms as separate languages. Tulu is widely considered one of the most rich and well organized for many reasons.

Found largely in Karnataka, it is spoken primarily within the Indian state. Dating back several hundred years, the language has developed numerous defining qualities. The Tulu people follow a saying which promotes leaving negative situations and finding newer, more positive ones. The language, however, is not as popular as others which means it could become endangered and extinct very soon. The influence of other mainstream languages is present danger for the Tulu people. With the right degree of awareness, we can help promote Tulu to more people who may appreciate it and its uniqueness. Today, it is spoken by nearly 1.8 million people around the globe. Large parts of the language are altered and changed constantly because it is commonly passed down through oral tradition. Oral traditions within Tulu have meant that certain phrases have not always maintained the same meaning or importance.

KONKANI LANGUAGE

Konkani is an Indo-Aryan language belonging to the Indo-European family of languages and is spoken by Konkani people along the western coast of India. It is one of the 22 scheduled languages mentioned in the 8th schedule of the Indian Constitution and the official language of the Indian state of Goa. The first Konkani inscription is dated 1187 A.D. It is a minority language in Karnataka, Maharashtra and Kerala, Dadra and Nagar Haveli, and Daman and Diu.

Konkani is a member of the southern Indo-Aryan language group. It retains elements of Proto-Dravidian structures and shows similarities with both western and eastern Indo-Aryan languages.

There are many fractured Konkani dialects, most of which are not mutually intelligible with one another.

Appellations

It is quite possible that Old Konkani was just referred to as *Prakrit* by its speakers. Among the inscriptions at the foot of the colossal statue of Bahubali at Shravanabelagola in Karnataka are two lines reading thus: (i) Sri Chamundaraje Karaviyale and (ii)

Sri Ganga raje sutthale karaviyale. The first line was inscribed circa 981 AD and the second line in 116-17 AD. The language of these lines is Konkani according to S.B. Kulkarni (former head of Department of Marathi, Nagpur University) and Jose Pereira (former professor, Fordham University, USA). Considering these arguments, these inscriptions at Sravanabelegola may be considered the earliest Konkani inscriptions in Devanagari script. Reference to the name *Konkani* is not found in literature prior to the 13th century. The first reference of the name *Konkani* is in "Abhanga 263" of the 13th century Marathi saint poet, Namadeva(1270–1350). Konkani has been known by a variety of names: *Canarim, Concanim, Gomantaki, Bramana,* and *Goani.* It is called *Amchi Bhas* (our language) by native speakers (*Amchi Gele* in Dakshina Kannada), and *Govi* or *Goenchi Bhas* by others. Learned Marathi speakers tend to call it *Gomantaki.*

Konkani was commonly referred to as *Lingua Canarim* by the Portuguese and *Lingua Brahmana* by Catholic missionaries. The Portuguese later started referring to Konkani as *Lingua Concanim.*

The name *Canarim* or *Lingua Canarim*, which is how the 16th century European Jesuit, Thomas Stephens refers to it in the title of his famous work *Arte da lingoa Canarim* has always been intriguing. It is possible that the term is derived from the Persian word for coast, *kinara*; if so, it would mean "the language of the coast". The problem is that this term overlaps with *Kanarese* or Kannada.

All the European authors, however, recognised two forms of the language in Goa: the plebeian, called *Canarim*, and the more regular (used by the educated classes), called *Lingua Canarim Brámana* or simply *Brámana de Goa.* The latter was the preferred choice of the Europeans, and also of other castes, for writing, sermons, and religious purposes.

History

Etymology

There are different views as to the origin of the word Konkan and hence Konkani

- The word Konkan comes from the Kukkana tribe, who were the original inhabitants of the land where Konkani originated.

Pre-history and early development

Konkani belongs to the Indo-Aryan language branch. It is inflexive, and less distant from Sanskrit as compared to other modern Indo-Aryan languages. Linguists describe Konkani as a fusion of variety of Prakrits. This could be attributed to the confluence of immigrants that the Konkan coast has witnessed over the years. Konkani developed with overall Sanskrit complexity and grammatical structure, which eventually developed into a lexical fund of its own. The second wave of Indo-Aryans is believed to have been accompanied by Dravidians from the Deccan plateau.

Goa and Konkan was ruled by the Konkan Mauryas and the Bhojas; as a result numerous migrations occurred from North, East and Western India. Immigrants spoke various vernaculars, which led to a mixture of features of Eastern and Western Prakrits. It was substantially influenced later by Magadhi Prakrit. The overtones of Pali (the liturgical language of the Buddhists) also played a very important role in the development of Konkani Apabhramsha grammar and vocabulary. A major number of linguistic innovations in Konkani are shared with Eastern Indo-Aryan languages like Bengali and Oriya, which have their roots in Magadhi.

Maharashtri was the official language of the Satavahana Empire that ruled Goa and Konkan in the early centuries of the Common Era. Under the patronage of the Satavahana Empire, Maharashtri became the most widespread Prakrit of its time. Studying early Maharashtri compilations, many linguists have called Konkani "the first-born daughter of Maharashtri". This old language that was prevalent contemporary to old Marathi is found to be distinct from its counterpart.

The Sauraseni impact on Konkani is not as prominent as that of Maharashtri. Very few Konkani words are found to follow the Sauraseni pattern. Konkani forms are rather more akin to Pali than the corresponding Sauraseni forms. The major Sauraseni influence on Konkani is the *ao* sound found at the end of many nouns in Sauraseni, which becomes *o* or *u* in Konkani. Examples include: *dando*, *suno*, *raakhano*, *dukh*, *rukhu*, *manisu* (from Prakrit), *dandao*, *sunnao*, *rakkhakao*, *dukkhao*, *vukkhao*, *vrukkhao*, and *mannisso*. Another example could be the sound of ण at the beginning of words; it is still retained in many Konkani words of archaic Shauraseni origin, such as णव (nine). Archaic Konkani born out of Shauraseni vernacular Prakrit at the earlier stage of the evolution (and later Maharashtri Prakrit), was commonly spoken until 875 AD, and at its later phase ultimately developed into Apabhramsha, which could be called a predecessor of old Konkani.

Goan Konkani

Entrance to Konkani section of the Golden Heart Emporium, Margao, Goa

- Under the ISO 639-3 classification, all the dialects of the

Konkani language except for those that come under Maharashtrian Konkani are collectively assigned the language code ISO 639:gom and called Goan Konkani. In this context, it includes dialects spoken outside the state of Goa, such as Mangalorean Konkani, Chitpavani Konkani Malvani Konkani and Karwari Konkani.

- In common usage, Goan Konkani refers collectively only to those dialects of Konkani spoken primarily in the state of Goa, e.g. the Antruz, Bardeskari and Saxtti dialects.

Organisations

There are organisations working for Konkani but, primarily, these were restricted to individual communities. The All India Konkani Parishadfounded on 8 July 1939, provided a common ground for Konkani people from all regions. A new organisation known as Vishwa Konkani Parishad, which aims to be an all-inclusive and pluralistic umbrella organisation for Konkanis around the world, was founded on 11 September 2005.

Mandd Sobhann is the premier organisation that is striving hard to preserve, promote, propagate, and enrich the Konkani language and culture.

World Konkani Centre, Mangalore

The Konkan Daiz Yatra, started in 1939 in Mumbai, is the oldest Konkani organisation. The Konkani Bhasha Mandal was born in Mumbai on 5 April 1942, during the Third Adhiveshan of All India Konkani Parishad. On 28 December 1984, Goa Konkani Akademi (GKA) was founded by the government of Goa to promote Konkani language, literature, and culture. The Thomas Stephens Konknni Kendr (TSKK) is a popular research institute based in the Goan capital Panaji. It works on issues related to the Konkani language, literature, culture, and education. The Dalgado Konkani Academy is a popular Konkani organisation based in Panaji.

The Konkani Triveni Kala Sangam is one more famed Konkani organisation in Mumbai, which is engaged in the vocation of patronising Konkani language through the theatre movement. The government of Karnataka established the Karnataka Konkani Sahitya Akademy on 20 April 1994. The Konkani Ekvott is an umbrella organisation of the Konkani bodies in Goa.

The First World Konkani Convention was held in Mangalore in December 1995. The Konkani Language and Cultural Foundation came into being immediately after the World Konkani Convention in 1995.

The World Konkani Centre built on a three-acre plot called Konkani Gaon (Konkani Village) at Shakti Nagar, Mangalore was inaugurated on 17 January 2009, "to serve as a nodal agency for the preservation and overall development of Konkani language, art, and culture involving all the Konkani people the world over."

Literature

During the Goa Inquisition which commenced in 1560, all books found in the Konkani language were burnt, and it is possible that old Konkani literature was destroyed as a consequence.

The earliest writer in the history of Konkani language known today is Krishnadas Shama from Quelossim in Goa. He began writing 25 April 1526, and he authored *Ramayana*, *Mahabharata*, and *Krishnacharitrakatha* in prose style. The manuscripts have not been found, although transliterations in Roman script are found in Braga in Portugal. The script used by him for his work is not known.

The first known printed book in Konkani was written by an English Jesuit priest, Fr. Thomas Stephens in 1622, and entitled *Doutrina Christam em Lingoa Bramana Canarim* (Old Portuguese for: *Christian Doctrine in the Canarese Brahman Language*). The first book exclusively on Konkani grammar, *Arte da Lingoa Canarim*, was printed in 1640 by Father Stephens in Portuguese.

5

Geography and Flora & Fauna

GEOGRAPHY

The state has three principal geographical zones:

1. The coastal region of Karavali
2. The hilly Malenadu region comprising the Western Ghats
3. The Bayaluseeme region comprising the plains of the Deccan plateau

The bulk of the state is in the Bayaluseeme region, the northern part of which is the second-largest arid region in India. The highest point in Karnataka is the Mullayanagiri hills in Chickmagalur district which has an altitude of 1,929 metres (6,329 ft). Some of the important rivers in Karnataka are Kaveri, Tungabhadra, Krishna, Malaprabha and the Sharavathi. A large number of dams and reservoirs are constructed across these rivers which richly add to the irrigation and hydel power generation capacities of the state.

Karnataka consists of four main types of geological formations — the *Archean complex* made up of Dharwad schists and granitic gneisses, the *Proterozoic* non-fossiliferous sedimentary formations of the Kaladgi and Bhima series, the *Deccan trappean and intertrappean deposits* and the tertiary and recent laterites and alluvial deposits. Significantly, about

60% of the state is composed of the *Archean complex*which consist of gneisses, granites and charnockite rocks. Laterite cappings that are found in many districts over the Deccan Traps were formed after the cessation of volcanic activity in the early tertiary period. Eleven groups of soil orders are found in Karnataka, viz. Entisols, Inceptisols, Mollisols, Spodosols, Alfisols, Ultisols, Oxisols, Aridisols, Vertisols, Andisols and Histosols. Depending on the agricultural capability of the soil, the soil types are divided into six types, *viz.* red, lateritic, black, alluvio-colluvial, forest and coastal soils.

Jog Falls, formed by Sharavathi River, are the second highest plunge waterfalls in India.

Karnataka experiences four seasons. The winter in January and February is followed by summer between March and May, the monsoon season between June and September and the post-monsoon season from October till December. Meteorologically, Karnataka is divided into three zones — coastal, north interior and south interior. Of these, the coastal zone receives the heaviest rainfall with an average rainfall of about 3,638.5 mm (143 in) per annum, far in excess of the state average of 1,139 mm (45 in). Agumbe in the Shivamogga district receives the second highest annual rainfall in India. The highest recorded temperature was 45.6 °C (114 °F) at Raichur and the lowest recorded temperature was 2.8 °C (37 °F) at Bidar.

About 38,724 km^2 (14,951 sq mi) of Karnataka (i.e. 20% of the state's geographic area) is covered by forests. The forests are classified as reserved, protected, unclosed, village and private forests. The percentage of forested area is slightly less than the all-India average of about 23%, and significantly less than the 33% prescribed in the National Forest Policy.

Geography of Karnataka

The Indian State of Karnataka is located 11°30' North and 18°30' North latitudes and 74° East and 78°30' East longitude. It is situated on a tableland where the Western and Eastern Ghat ranges converge into the complex, in the western part of the Deccan Peninsular region of India.

The State is bounded by Maharashtra and Goa States in the north and northwest; by the Arabian Sea in the west; by Kerala and Tamil Nadu States in the south and by the States of Andhra Pradesh and Telangana in the east. Karnataka extends to about 750 km from north to south and about 400 km from east to west.

Karnataka is situated in the Deccan Plateau and is bordered by the Arabian Sea to the west, Goa to the northwest, Maharashtrato the north, Andhra Pradesh and Telangana to the east, Tamil Nadu to the southeast, and Kerala to the southwest. It is situated at the angle where the Western Ghats and Eastern Ghats of South India converge into the Nilgiri hills. The highest point in Karnataka is the Mullayanagiri hill in Chikkamagaluru district which has an altitude of 1,929 metres (6,329 ft) above sea level.

LANDFORMS OF KARNATAKA

The state has three principal physical zones;

- The coastal strip, called Karavalli, between the Western Ghats and the Arabian Sea, which is lowland, with moderate to high rainfall levels. This strip is around 320 km in length and 48–64 km wide.
- The Western Ghats, called Malenadu, a mountain range islands from the Arabian Sea, rising to about 900 m average height, and with moderate to high rainfall levels.
- The Deccan Plateau, called Bayalu Seeme, comprising the main inland region of the state, which is drier and verging on the semi-arid. The humidity in these plains or maidans never exceeds 50%.

Karnataka has one of the highest average elevations of Indian states at 1,500 feet. The highest recorded temperature was 45.6 °C (114.08 °F) at Raichur on May 23, 1928. The lowest recorded temperature was 2.8 °C (37.04 °F) at Bidar on December 16, 1918.

Area and population

Karnataka has a total land area of 191,791 km^2 and accounts for 5.83% of the total area of the country (measured at 3,288,000 km^2). This puts it in seventh place in terms of size. With a population of 6,11,30,704, it occupies eighth place in terms of population. The population density which stands at 319 persons per km^2 is lower than the all-India average of 382.

Mineral resources

Karnataka is rich in its mineral wealth which is distributed fairly evenly across the state. Karnataka's Geological Survey department started in 1880 is one of the oldest in the country. Rich deposits of asbestos, bauxite, chromite, dolomite, gold, iron ore, kaolin, limestone, magnesite, Manganese, ochre, quartz and silica sand are found in the state. Karnataka is also a major producer of felsite, moulding sand (63%) and fuchsite quartzite (57%) in the country.

Karnataka has two major centers of gold mining in the state at Kolar and Raichur. These mines produce about 3000 kg of gold per annum which accounts for almost 84% of the country's production. Karnataka has very rich deposits of high grade iron and manganese ores to the tune of 1,000 million tonnes. Most of the iron ores are concentrated around the Bellary-Hospet region. Karnataka with a granite rock spread of over 4200 km^2 is also famous for its Ornamental Granites with different hues.

Geology

According to Radhakrishnan and Vaidyanadhan (1997), there are four main types of geological formations in Karnataka:

- *The Archean complex made up of Dharwad schists and granitic gneisses*: These cover around 60% of the area of the state and consist of gneisses, granites and charnockite rocks. Some of the minerals found in this region are dolomite, limestone, gabbro, quartzite, pyroxenite, manganese and iron ores and metabasalt.
- *The Proterozoic non-fossiliferous sedimentary formations of the Kaladgi and Bhima series*: The Kaladgi series has horizontal rocks consists of sandstone, metabasalt, limestone, trapstone that run for 160 km in the districts of Belgaum, Raichur, Dharwad and Bijapur districts. The Bhima series that is present on either side of the Bhima River consists of rocks containing sandstone, limestone and shale and this is present in the Gulbarga and Bijapur districts.
- *The Deccan trappean and intertrappean deposits*: This is a part of the Deccan traps which were formed by the accumulation of basaltic lava. This is made up of greyish to black augite-basalt.
- *The tertiary and recent laterites and alluvial deposits*: Laterite capping are found over the Deccan Traps and were formed after the cessation of volcanic activity in the early tertiary period. These are found in many districts in the Deccan plateau and also in the coast.

Soil types

Eleven groups of soil orders are found in Karnataka viz. Entisols, Inceptisols, Mollisols, Spodosols, Alfisols, Ultisols, Oxisols, Aridisols, Vertisols, Andisols and Histosols. Depending on the agricultural capability of the soil, the soil types are divided into six types viz., Red, lateritic (lateritic soil is found in bidar and kolar district), black, alluvio-colluvial, forest and coastal soils. The common types of soil groups found in Karnataka are:

- Red soils: Red gravelly loam soil, Red loam soil, Red gravelly clay soil, Red clay soil
- Black cotton soil: gravelly soil,loose, black soil , basalt deposits
- Lateritic soils: Lateritic gravelly soil, Lateritic soil
- Black soils: Deep black soil, Medium deep black soil, Shallow black soil
- Alluvio-Colluvial Soils: Non-saline, saline and sodic
- Forest soils: Brown forest soil
- Coastal soils: Coastal laterite soil, Coastal alluvial soil

WATER RESOURCES

With a surface water potential of about 102 kilometers, Karnataka accounts for about six percent of the country's surface water resources. Around 60% of this is provided by the west flowing rivers while the remaining comes from the east flowing rivers. There are seven river basins in all formed by the Godavari, Cauvery, Krishna, the west-flowing rivers, North Pennar River, South Pennar, and Palar.

Water Falls in Karnataka

Lot of WaterFalls in Karnataka.

- kadambi Falls
- Kalhatti Falls
- Anashi Falls
- Chakra River
- Vibhooti Falls

- Onake Abbi Falls
- Hanumangundi Falls
- chelavara Falls
- Kadra Falls
- gootlu Falls
- hidlumane Falls
- Godchinamalaki Falls
- Abbey Falls
- Bandaje Falls
- Barkana Falls
- Chunchanakatte Falls
- Devaragundi Falls
- Gokak Falls
- Hebbe Falls
- Irupu Falls
- Jaladurga Falls
- Jog Falls
- Kalhatti Falls
- Kunchikal Falls
- Magod Falls
- Mallalli Falls
- Muthyalamaduvu Falls
- Sathodi Falls
- Shivanasamudra Falls
- Shivganga Falls
- Sirimane Falls
- Vajrapoha Falls
- Varapoha Falls
- Unchalli Falls

East flowing rivers

26 east-flowing rivers.

- Amarja

- Arkavathy River
- Agrani River
- Bhadra River
- Chakra River
- Dandavathi
- Doni River
- Ghataprabha River
- Hemavati River
- Hiranyakeshi River
- Honnuhole River
- Kabini River
- Kaveri River
- Kagina River
- Kedaka River
- Krishna River
- Kubja River
- Lakshmana Tirtha River
- Malaprabha River
- Palar River
- Panchagangavalli River
- Penner River
- Ponnaiyar River
- Shimsha
- South Pennar River
- Tunga River
- Tungabhadra River
- Varada
- Vedavathi River
- Vrishabhavathi River

West flowing rivers

10 west-flowing rivers, providing 60% of state's inland water resources.

- Gangavalli River
- Aghanashini River
- Kali River
- Kumaradhara River
- Mahadai River
- Shambavi
- Varahi River
- Souparnika River
- Sharavathi River
- Netravati River
- Gurupura River
- seethanadhi river

Reservoirs

- Lalbahadur shastri sagar, Alamatti
- Basava Sagar Reservoir
- Navilu theerth Reservoir
- Ghataprabha Reservoir
- Dhupdal Reservoir
- Tungabhadra dam, Hospete
- Linganamakki
- Bhadra reservoir
- Krishna Raja Sagara
- Tippagondanahalli Reservoir
- Harangi dam
- Hemavathi Reservoir
- Karanja Reservoir, Bidar

Lakes

- Lakes in Davangere (Shanthisagara biggest lake in India)
- Lakes in Bangalore
- Mysore city lakes
- Unkal lake, Hubli

- Belgaum Fort Lake
- Heggeri Lake, Haveri
- Hagari Jalashaya , Malavi
- Sharanabasava lake , Kalaburagi

Climate

Karnataka has the following four seasons in the year:

- The winter season from January to February
- The summer season from March to May
- The monsoon season from May to September
- The post-monsoon season from October to December.

The post-monsoon (period of retreating) and winter seasons are generally pleasant over the entire state. The months April and May are hot, very dry and generally uncomfortable. Weather tends to be oppressive during June due to high humidity and temperature.

The next three months (July, August and September) are somewhat comfortable due to reduced day temperature although the humidity continue to be very high. The highest recorded temperature was 45.6 °C (114 °F) at Raichur on May 23, 1928. The lowest recorded temperature was 2.8 °C (37 °F) C at Bidar on December 16, 1918.

Karnataka is divided into three meteorological zones:

- *Coastal Karnataka*: This zone comprises the districts of Uttara Kannada, Udupi and Dakshina Kannada. It is a region of heavy rainfall and receives an average rainfall of 3638.5 mm per annum. far in excess of rest of state.
- *North Interior Karnataka*: This zone comprises the districts of Belgaum, Bidar, Bijapur, Bagalkot, Haveri, Gadag, Dharwad, Gulbarga, Koppal, Bellary and Raichur Districts. This is an arid zone and receives only 711.5 mm of average rainfall per annum.
- *South Interior Karnataka*: The rest of the districts of Karnataka falls into this zone. This zone receives 1064.8 mm of average rainfall per annum.

RAINFALL IN KARNATAKA

The state of Karnataka in India has a bittersweet relationship with rains. While its regions of Malnad and Coastal Karnataka receive copious amount of rainfall; its north Bayaluseemae region in the Deccan Plateau is one of the most arid regions in the country.

Most of the rains received in the state is during the monsoon season. Being an agrarian economy with a large percentage of its citizens engaged in agriculture, the failure of rains can have a crippling effect on the economy of the state.

Apart from the benefits in agriculture, the Government of Karnataka has tried to avail other benefits of rainfall using scientific methods. An example of this is the project, *Rainwater Harvesting in Rural Karnataka* which is initiated by the Karnataka State Council for Science and Technology and is one of the largest rainwater harvesting projects in the world.Agumbe in the Shimoga district is known as one of the places with the highest annual rainfall in India.

Heavy rains show the full might of Jog Falls in Shimoga district

Importance

The economy of Karnataka is mainly agrarian and most of it is dependent on the rainfall; mainly the southwest monsoon.

The extent of arid land in the state is second only to Rajasthan. Only 26.5% of sown area (30,900 km^2) is subjected to irrigation and hence the rest of the cultivated land is entirely dependent on rainfall.

Rainfall also influences the quantity of water available in the rivers which in turn influences the amount of drinking water available to the population and the amount of electricity that can be generated in the hydroelectric power stations in the state.

The importance of rainfall is such that Karnataka sometimes had to resort to costly artificial methods like cloud seeding in order to induce rain artificially. Rainfall is also crucial to recharge the depleting ground water and Karnataka has come up with innovative methods like rainwater harvesting in order to solve the drinking water scarcity in the state.

Rainwater harvesting

Karnataka is a pioneer in the concept of rainwater harvesting with The Karnataka State Council for Science and Technology (KSCST) implementing one of the largest rainwater harvesting projects in the world.

23683 schools in rural Karnataka were selected for this project with the main goal of providing drinking water by using the method of rooftop harvesting. In this project, rainwater collected on the rooftop is channeled through a system of PVC pipes and stored in an enclosed surface tank.

The pipeline consists of a first-flush filter which flushes out the first rainfall along with other contaminants that may exist on the roof and then subsequent cleaner rainwater is allowed to pass on to the tank. A sand bed filter is used to further eliminate impurities in the water before it gets collected in the tank. Further precautions are taken to prevent dust and insects from entering the tank.

Consequences

Deficient rainfall

A year of deficient rainfall leads to the following consequences:

- Agricultural output will be impacted: While this has a direct impact on the economy of the state, it also leads to other social issues like the suicide of farmers. Due to the crop failure, the farmers would not be in a position to repay the loans they had taken for agriculture and few of them take an extreme step of suicide.
- Drinking water scarcity: A lot of towns and cities in Karnataka are dependent on rivers for the supply of drinking water and any deficiency in rainfall leads to lesser amount of drinking water being supplied to the homes.
- Shortage of electricity: Deficient rainfall leads to a drop in the amount of electricity produced by hydroelectric projects and hence drastic measures like compulsory power cuts have to be employed to counter this shortage.

Excess rainfall

Heavy rains can lead to a significant loss of life and property and also cause damage to the crops. Excess rains also cause an impact in major cities with inundated roads causing traffic jams.

An example of this was in the year 2005 when the Madivala lake overflowed on to the Hosur Road in Bangalore forcing many schools and offices to close.

Rainfall distribution

The average annual rainfall in Karnataka is 1248 mm. The state is divided into three meteorological zones viz. North Interior Karnataka, South Interior Karnataka and Coastal Karnataka. Coastal Karnataka with an average annual rainfall of 3456 mm is one of the most rainy regions in the country. Contrasting this, the region of South Interior Karnataka and North Interior Karnataka receive only 1286 and 731 mm of average annual rainfall.

Districts

The average annual rainfall in the districts of Karnataka varies from 562 mm in the Bagalkot district to 4119 mm in the Udupi District. Bagalkot, Chitradurga and Koppal are the districts which receive the least rainfall whereas Udupi, Dakshina Kannada, Uttara Kannada, Hassan, Kodagu, Chickmagalur and Shivamogga districts receive the heaviest rainfall.

SUB-DIVISIONS

There are 30 districts in Karnataka:

- Bagalkote
- Bangalore Rural
- Bangalore Urban
- Belgaum
- Ballari
- Bidar
- Chamarajanagar
- Chikkaballapur
- Chikkamagaluru
- Chitradurga
- Dakshina Kannada
- Davanagere
- Dharwad
- Gadag
- Gulbarga
- Hassan
- Haveri
- Kodagu
- Kolar
- Koppal
- Mandya

- Mysore
- Raichur
- Ramanagara
- Shimoga
- Tumakuru
- Udupi
- Uttara Kannada
- Vijayapur
- Yadgir

Each district is governed by a district commissioner or district magistrate. The districts are further divided into sub-divisions, which are governed by sub-divisional magistrates; sub-divisions comprise blocks containing *panchayats* (village councils) and town municipalities. At the 2011 census, Karnataka's ten largest cities, sorted in order of decreasing population, were Bangalore, Hubli-Dharwad, Mysuru, Gulbarga, Belgaum, Mangalore, Davangere, Bellary, Vijayapur and Shimoga.

WILDLIFE OF KARNATAKA

Indian roller, (**Coracias benghalensis**)*, the state bird*

Young sapling of sandalwood (**Santalum album**)*, the state tree*

The state of Karnataka in South India has a rich diversity of flora and fauna. It has a recorded forest area of 38720 km which constitutes 20.19% of the total geographical area of the state. These forests support 25% of the elephant population and 20% of the tiger population of India. Many regions of Karnataka are still unexplored and new species of flora and fauna are still found. The Western Ghats mountains in the western region of Karnataka are a biodiversity hotspot. Two sub-clusters of the Western Ghats, Talacauvery and Kudremukh in Karnataka, are in a tentative list of sites that could be designated as World Heritage Sites by UNESCO. The Bandipur and Nagarahole national parks which fall outside these subclusters were included in the Nilgiri biosphere reserve in 1986, a UNESCO designation. Biligiriranga Hills in Karnataka is a place where Eastern Ghats meets Western Ghats. The state bird and state animal of Karnataka are Indian roller and the Indian elephantrespectively. The state tree and state flower are sandalwood (*Santalum album*) and lotus respectively. Karnataka is home to 406+ tigers (around 12% of tigers in world).

National parks in Karnataka

The tiger Panthera tigris. *Karnataka has around 20% of the tiger population in India*

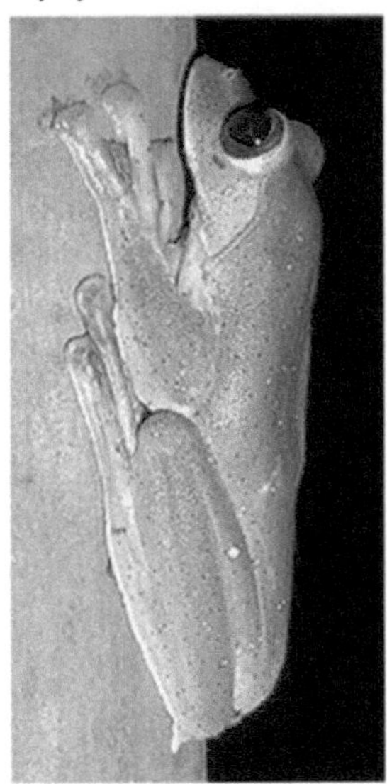

The Malabar gliding frog (Rhacophorus malabaricus) *found in the Western Ghats*

Anshi National Park

This park is present in the Uttara Kannada district and spreads over an area of 250 km. The altitude varies from 27 metres (89 ft) to 937 metres (3,074 ft), and temperatures from 15.5 °C to 45 °C. Average annual rainfall is about 4,700 millimetres (185 in) .

- Flora: The area has semi-evergreen and evergreen forests. Some common tree species in the area are *Calophylluum tomentosa*, *Calophyllum wightianum*, *Garcina cambogia*, *Garcina morealla*, *Knema attenuata*, *Hopea wightiana*, *Tetrameles nudiflora*, *Alstonia scholaris*, *Flacourtia montana*, *Machilis macarantha*, *Carallia brachiata*, *Artocarpus hirsutus*, *Artocarpus lacoocha* and *Cinnamomum zeylanicum*.
- Fauna: Mammals in the park include Indian elephant, gaur, wild boar, sambar, chevrotain, muntjac, chital, gray langur, bonnet macaque, slender loris, Bengal tiger, jungle cat, Indian leopard, leopard cat, small Indian civet, common mongoose, golden jackal, dhol, sloth bear, Malabar giant squirrel, grizzled giant squirrel, Indian giant flying squirrel, and Indian crested porcupine. King cobra, python, cobra, rat snake, viper and krait are among the snakes that inhabit the park. Interesting birds include the great hornbill, Malabar pied hornbill and Ceylon frogmouth.

Wildlife sanctuaries

Karnataka also has the following 18 wildlife sanctuaries:

- Adichunchanagiri Wildlife Sanctuary: This is located in Mandya district and is spread over 0.88 square kilometres (0.34 sq mi). This was created mainly for the conservation of peacocks. It also houses nearly 250 species of birds.
- Arabithittu Wildlife Sanctuary: This is located in Mysore district and is spread over 13.5 square kilometres (5.2 sq mi). This park consists of eucalyptus and sandalwood plantations. Leopard, fox and spotted deer are some of

the animal species found here. Also around 230 species of birds have been observed here over the years.

*Spot-billed pelican, (***Pelecanus philippensis***), a bird found in the bird sanctuaries of Karnataka*

- Biligiriranga Swamy Temple Wildlife Sanctuary: This is located in the Chamarajanagar district and is spread over 539.58 square kilometres (208.33 sq mi). Some of the species of flora found here are *Anogeissus latifolia*, *Grewia tilaefolia* and *Syzygium cumini*. Species of mammals include elephants, tigers, leopards, sloth bear, gaur, barking deer and sambar. Among the 215 species of birds found here include Nilgiri wood pigeon, Malabar whistling thrush, yellow-throated bulbul, peregrine falcon, rufous-bellied hawk-eagle. An endangered amphibian, *Icthyophis ghytinosus* has been reported in this sanctuary.
- Bhadra Wildlife Sanctuary: This is located between the Chikkamagaluru and Shimoga districts and is spread over 492.46 square kilometres (190.14 sq mi). Common species of flora include *Lagerstromia lanceolata*, *Adina cordifolia* and *Careya arborea*. Mammals include tiger,

leopard, elephant, gaur, slender loris and pangolin. Among the bird species found here are ruby-throated bulbul, shama, Malabar whistling thrush and paradise flycatcher.

- Brahmagiri Wildlife Sanctuary: This is located in Kodagu district and is spread over an area of 181.80 square kilometres (70.19 sq mi). The evergreen forests in this sanctuary include species like *Cinnamomum zeylancium*, *Cedrela toona* and *Alstonia scholaris*. Bamboos are dominant here and include species like *Bambusa bambos* and *Dendrocalamus strictus*. Mammals include elephant, gaur, tiger, jungle cat, bonnet macaque and Nilgiri marten. Also around 300 species of birds have been observed here over the years.
- Cauvery Wildlife Sanctuary: It is spread across the districts of Bangalore, Mysore and Mandya and is spread over 102.59 square kilometres (39.61 sq mi). Dry deciduous trees found in this park include species like *Terminalia arjuna* and *Syzgium cumini*. Animal species found in this park include leopard, elephant, sambar and common otter. This is also one of the last refuge of the highly endangered grizzled giant squirrel in Karnataka. Also around 300 species of birds have been observed here over the years. This sanctuary is also famous for mahseer fish (*Tor* species).
- Dandeli Wildlife Sanctuary: This is located in Uttara Kannada district and is spread over 475.02 square kilometres (183.41 sq mi). Common tree species found here are *Dalbergia latifolia*, *Terminalia paniculata*, T. Tomentosa and Vitex altissima. Mammal species include elephant, gaur, wild boar, slender loris, Malabar giant squirrel and barking deer.
- Daroji Sloth Bear Sanctuary: This is located in Bellary district and is spread over 55.87 square kilometres (21.57 sq mi). This sanctuary was mainly created for the conservation of sloth bears.
- Malai Mahadeshwara Wildlife Sanctuary: Spread over 906 square kilometers (349.8 sq mi), MM Hills wildlife

sanctuary came to being on 7th May 2013. Contiguous with BRT Tiger Reserve and Cauvery Wildlife Sanctuary, the sanctuary boasts of tiger, elephant, leopard, dhole, sambar, barking deer and others. The sanctuary is located in Chamarajanagar district, Kollegala taluk.

- Melukote Temple Wildlife Sanctuary: This is located in Mandya district and is spread over 45.82 square kilometres (17.69 sq mi). An endangered species of flora, *Cycas circinalis* is found here. Mammal species include wolf, leopard, blackbuck and pangolin. Also around 230 species of birds have been observed here over the years.
- Mookambika Wildlife Sanctuary: This is located in Udupi district and is spread over 247 square kilometres (95 sq mi). Some of the tree species found here are *Dipterocarpus indicus*, *Calophyllum tomentosum* and *Hopea parviflora*. An endangered species of climber *Coscinium fenestratum* has been recorded here. Slender loris, lion-tailed macaque, sambar and chital are some of the animals found here. The endangered cane turtle is also found here.
- Nugu Wildlife Sanctuary: This is located in Mysore district and is spread over 30.32 square kilometres (11.71 sq mi). Common species of flora include *Emblica officinalis*, *Santalum album* and *Dendrocalamus strictus*. Mammals include elephant, gaur, leopard, spotted deer and common palm civet.
- Pushpagiri Wildlife Sanctuary: This is located in Kodagu district and is spread over 102.59 square kilometres (39.61 sq mi). Some species of flora found here are *Hopea parviflora*, *Schefflera capitata*, *Xanthalis tomentosa* and *Ochlandra rheedii*. Mammals include elephant, tiger, slender loris, Nilgiri marten and bonnet macaque. Also around 230 species of birds have been observed here over the years. Bird species include great pied hornbill, Malabar trogon and Nilgiri blackbird.
- Ranibennur Blackbuck Sanctuary: This is located in Haveri district and is spread over 119.00 square kilometres (45.95 sq mi). Eucalyptus is the dominant species of trees

found here. *Cassia fistula, Prosopsis julifora* and *Zizyphus mauritania* are other tree species found here. This sanctuary was created mainly for the conservation of blackbucks. This sanctuary is also a habitat for the endangered great Indian bustard.

- Sharavathi Valley Wildlife Sanctuary: This is located in Shimoga district and is spread over 431.23 square kilometres (166.50 sq mi). *Dipterocarpus indicus, Caryota urens* and *Dillenia pentagyna* are some of the species of flora found here. Tiger, leopard, mouse deer, bonnet macaque and common langur are some of the animal species found here. Snakes are commonly found here. Paradise flycatcher, racket-tailed drongo and blue-throated barbet are some of the bird species found here.
- Shettihalli Wildlife Sanctuary: This is located in Shimoga district and is spread over 395.60 square kilometres (152.74 sq mi). *Cassia fistula, Kydia calycina* and *Wrightia tinctoria*are some of the species of flora found here. Tiger, leopard, bonnet macaque and Malabar giant squirrel are some of the animal species found here.
- Someshwara Wildlife Sanctuary: This is located in Udupi district and is spread over 88.40 square kilometres (34.13 sq mi). *Machilus macrantha, Lophopetalum wightanium* and *Artocarpus hirsuta* are some of the species of flora found here. Tiger, leopard, lion-tailed macaque and spotted deer are some of the animal species found here.
- Talakaveri Wildlife Sanctuary: This is located in Kodagu district and is spread over 105.00 square kilometres (40.54 sq mi). *Albizzia lebbek, Artocarpus lakoocha, Dysoxylum malabaricum* and *Mesua ferrea* are some of the species of flora found here. Clawless otter, elephant, tiger, striped-necked mongoose and mouse deer are some of the animal species found here. Also around 300 species of birds have been observed here over the years. Fairy bluebird, Malabar trogon and broadbill roller are some of the avian species found.

Bird sanctuaries

*A pair of painted storks(***Mycteria leucocephala***) in Ranganathittu Bird Sanctuary*

- Attiveri Bird Sanctuary: This is located in Uttara Kannada district and is spread over 2.23 km. white ibis, little cormorant, pied kingfisher, common grey hornbill are some of the bird species found here.
- Gudavi Bird Sanctuary: This is located in Shimoga district and is spread over 0.73 km. The tree species that dominate this sanctuary are *Vitex leucoxylon* and *Phyllanthus polyphyllus*. 191 species of birds are recorded here including white ibis, pheasant-tailed jacana, purple moorhen and little grebe.
- Ranganathittu Bird Sanctuary: This is located in Mandya district and is spread over 0.67 km. Among the tree species found here, is the unique *Iphigenia mysorensis*. Other tree species include *Derris indica* and *Barringtonia racemosa*. This sanctuary houses nearly 170 birds. Birds like cormorants, darter, white ibis, great stone plover, cliff swallow, spoonbills, lesser whistling teal roost here all through the year.

- Mandagadde Bird Sanctuary: It is located near the little village Mandagadde which is 30 km from the Shimoga town and is based on a small island on the Tunga River. It is mainly visited by migratory birds like median egret (*Egretta intermedia*), the little cormorant (*Microcarbo niger*), and the darter or snake bird (*Aninga nufa*).
- Kaggaladu Heronry: This is located in Tumkur district and is one of the largest painted stork sanctuaries in South India. Some of the birds that nest here are painted storks, grey herons, pelicans, black stilts and ducks.
- Kokrebellur Pelicanry: This is located in the town of Kokkare Bellur in Mandya district and is a haven for avian species like grey or spot-billed pelican (*Pelecanus philippensis*) and painted stork (*Mycteria leucocephala*). In fact the word *Kokkare* means stork in the Kannadalanguage. Apart from pelicans and storks, 250 species of birds have been sighted here.
- Magadi Bird Sanctuary: Magadi Bird Sanctuary created at the Magadi tank, in Magadi village of Shirahatti Taluk, Gadag district. It is one of the Biodiversity hotspots of Karnataka, in North Karnataka. From Gadag it is 26 km, it is located on Gadag-Bangalore Road, from Shirahatti it is 8 km, and from Lakshmeshwara 11 km. Bar-headed goose is one of the bird migrates to Magadi wetlands of Gadag district. Normally birds eat fish, amphibians, molluscs, snakes etc., but migratory birds eating agricultural produce is both interesting and curious too. Winter habitat is on cultivation, it feeds on barley, rice and wheat and damage crops.
- Bankapura Peacock Sanctuary: This is located in Haveri district and spread over an area of 139.10 acres (0.5629 km). This sanctuary was created mainly for the conservation of peacocks.
- Bonal Bird Sanctuary : This is located about 10 km from Shorapur city in Yadgir district.
- Ramadevarabetta Vulture Sanctuary: This is located in

Ramanagara and is home of the critically endangered Long-billed vulture (Gyps indicus).

- Ghataprabha Bird Sanctuary: This is located in Belgaum district and is spread over 20.78 square kilometres (8.02 sq mi). This sanctuary is known for migratory birds like Demoiselle crane and European white stork.

Endangered species

Shorea roxburghii, *an endangered rainforest tree found in Karnataka*

Karnataka is the home of few critically endangered species of flora that include evergreen trees like *Dipterocarpus bourdilloni*, *Hopea erosa* and *Hopea jacobi*, *Croton lawianus* (a small tree) and *Pinnatella limbata* (a type of moss). Some of the critically endangered species of fauna found in Karnataka include *Gyps indicus* (the Indian vulture) and two species of frogs, *Indirana gundia* (found only in Gundia range, Sakleshpur) and *Micrixalus kottigeharensis* (found only near Kottigehara, Chikkamagaluru district).

Some of the endangered species of flora include evergreen trees like *Cynometra bourdillonii*, *Cynometra travancorica*, *Hopea glabra*, *Hopea parviflora*, *Hopea ponga*, *Hopea racophloea*, *Hopea wightiana*, *Shorea roxburghii* and *Tarenna agumbensis* and flowering plants like *Glochidion pauciflorum*, *Glochidion tomentosum*, *Ixora lawsoni* and *Syzygium stocksii*. Other endangered trees found in Karnataka include *Isonandra stocksii*, *Kingiodendron pinnatum*, *Maesa velutina*, *Myristica magnifica*, *Rapanea striata* and *Xylosma latifolium*.

Endangered species of fauna found in Karnataka include the Bengal tiger, Indian elephant, lion-tailed macaque, olive ridley turtle and dhole, the Indian wild dog. Many endangered species of amphibians are found here including frogs, *Indirana brachytarsus*, *Microhyla sholigari*, *Minervarya sahyadris*, *Nyctibatrachus aliciae*, *Nyctibatrachus hussaini*, *Nyctibatrachus sanctipalustris*, *Philautus charius*, *Philautus wynaadensis*, *Ramanella mormorata* and *Rhacophorus lateralis* and a toad, *Bufo beddomii*. Other endangered species of fauna include *Hipposideros hypophyllus* (the Kolar leaf-nosed bat) and *Pseudomulleria dalyi* (a mollusc).

FLORA AND FAUNA

Karnataka has a rich diversity of flora and fauna. It has a recorded forest area of 38,720 km (14,950 sq mi) which constitutes 20.19% of the total geographical area of the state. These forests support 25% of the elephant and 10% of the tiger population of India. Many regions of Karnataka are as yet unexplored, so new species of flora and fauna are found periodically. The Western Ghats, a biodiversity hotspot, includes the western region of Karnataka. Two sub-clusters in the Western Ghats, viz. Talacauvery and Kudremukh, both in Karnataka, are on the tentative list of World Heritage Sites of UNESCO. The Bandipur and Nagarahole National Parks, which fall outside these subclusters, were included in the Nilgiri Biosphere Reserve in 1986, a UNESCO designation. The Indian roller and the Indian elephant are recognised as the state bird and animal while sandalwood and the lotus are recognised as the state tree and flower respectively. Karnataka has five national parks: Anshi, Bandipur, Bannerghatta, Kudremukh and Nagarhole. It also has 27 wildlife sanctuaries of which seven are bird sanctuaries.

The state bird, Indian roller

Bengal tigers at Bannerghatta National Park near Bangalore

Wild animals that are found in Karnataka include the elephant, the tiger, the leopard, the gaur, the sambar deer, the chital or spotted deer, the muntjac, the bonnet macaque, the slender loris, the common palm civet, the small Indian civet, the sloth bear, the dhole, the striped hyena and the golden jackal. Some of the birds found here are the great hornbill, the Malabar pied hornbill, the Ceylon frogmouth, herons, ducks, kites, eagles, falcons, quails, partridges, lapwings, sandpipers, pigeons, doves, parakeets, cuckoos, owls, nightjars, swifts, kingfishers, bee-eaters and munias. Some species of trees found in Karnataka are *Callophyllum tomentosa*, *Callophyllum wightianum*, *Garcina cambogia*, *Garcina morealla*, *Alstonia scholaris*, *Flacourtia montana*, *Artocarpus hirsutus*, *Artocarpus lacoocha*, *Cinnamomum zeylanicum*, *Grewia tilaefolia*, *Santalum album*, *Shorea talura*, *Emblica officinalis*, *Vitex altissima* and *Wrightia tinctoria*. Wildlife in Karnataka is threatened by poaching, habitat destruction, human-wildlife conflict and pollution.

Flora and fauna of Karnataka, Indian Flora and Fauna

Flora and fauna of Karnataka are diverse and comprise of plants, animals, birds, reptiles, etc. Flora of Karnataka comprises of species like eucalyptus, teak and rosewood. Fauna of Karnataka comprises of species like leopard, gaur and wild pig.

Teak Trees

Flora and fauna of Karnataka are representatives of the rich biodiversity in the state. Wildlife in Karnataka is preserved in the protected areas of the state like national parks, wildlife sanctuaries and bird sanctuaries. There are 5 national parks and 30 sanctuaries in Karnataka.

Areas Protecting Flora and Fauna of Karnataka

The important national parks protecting the flora and fauna of Karnataka are Anshi National Park, Bandipur National Park, Bannerghatta National Park, Kudremukh National Park and Nagarhole National Park. Some of the wildlife sanctuaries of Karnataka are Biligiri Rangaswamy Temple Wildlife Sanctuary, Adichunchanagiri Peacock Sanctuary, Brahmagiri Wildlife Sanctuary and CauveryWildlife Sanctuary.

Elephants

Some of the bird sanctuaries of Karnataka are Attiveri Bird Sanctuary, Bonal Bird Sanctuary, Magadi Bird Sanctuary and Gudavi Bird Sanctuary.

Flora of Karnataka

The recorded forest of Karnataka encloses an area of about 43,356.47 square kilometers. It covers about 22.61 percent of the total geographical area of the state. Evergreen and semi-evergreen forest, moist deciduous forest, dry deciduous forest, scrub and thorny forestand un-wooded forest like grassland are found in Karnataka. Eucalyptus trees are found in abundance in the Western Ghats. Teak, rosewoodand casuarina beautify Karnataka.

Great Indian Hornbill

Other tree species found here are *Iphigenia Mysorensis, Derris Indica, Barringtonia Racemosa, Cassia Fistula, Prosopsis Julifora, Dipterocarpus Indicus, Caryota Urens, Dillenia Pentagyna* and *Zizyhus Mauritania.* The common species of flora include *Lagerstromia Lanceolata, Adina Cordifolia, Careya Arborea, Dalbergia Latifolia, Terminalia Paniculata, T. Tomentosa* and *Vitex Altissima.*

Fauna of Karnataka

In the forests of Karnataka, there are about 25 percent of elephants and about 20 percent of tigers. Mammals such as leopard, slender loris, gaur, wild pig, pangolin, Malabar giant squirrel, mouse deer, bonnet macaque, common langur and barking deer are found in Karnataka. The bird species found in the state are ruby throated bulbul, Indian shama, Malabar whistling thrush, orange headed trush, paradise flycatcher, great Indian hornbill, cormorant, darter, white ibis, great stone plover, cliff swallow, spoonbill, lesser whistling teal, open billed stork, painted stork, thick-knee, stony plover, pied kingfisher, common kingfisher, racket-tailed drongo and blue throated barbet. Reptiles like crocodile, tortoise, lizard, chameleon, gecko and snake are found in Karnataka.

6

Economy

ECONOMY

Karnataka had an estimated GSDP (Gross State Domestic Product) of about US$115.86 billion in the 2014–15 fiscal year. The state registered a GSDP growth rate of 7% for the year 2014–2015. Karnataka's contribution to India's GDP in the year 2014–15 was 7.54%. With GDP growth of 17.59% and per capita GDP growth of 16.04%, Karnataka is on the 6th position among all states and union territories. In an employment survey conducted for the year 2013–2014, the unemployment rate in Karnataka was 1.8% compared to the national rate of 4.9%. In 2011–2012, Karnataka had an estimated poverty ratio of 20.91% compared to the national ratio of 21.92%.

Nearly 56% of the workforce in Karnataka is engaged in agriculture and related activities. A total of 12.31 million hectares of land, or 64.6% of the state's total area, is cultivated. Much of the agricultural output is dependent on the southwest monsoon as only 26.5% of the sown area is irrigated.

Karnataka is the manufacturing hub for some of the largest public sector industries in India, including Hindustan Aeronautics Limited, National Aerospace Laboratories, Bharat Heavy Electricals Limited, Bharat Earth Movers Limited and HMT (formerly Hindustan Machine Tools), which are based in Bangalore. Many of India's premier science and technology research centres, such as Indian Space Research Organisation, Central Power Research Institute, Bharat Electronics Limited and the Central Food Technological Research Institute, are also headquartered in Karnataka. Mangalore Refinery and Petrochemicals Limited is an oil refinery, located in Mangalore.

The state has also begun to invest heavily in solar power centred on the Pavagada Solar Park. As of December 2017, the state has installed an estimated 2.2 gigwatts of block solar panelling and in January 2018 announced a tender to generate a further 1.2 gigawatts in the coming years: Karnataka Renewable Energy Development suggests that this will be based on 24 separate systems (or 'blocks') generating 50 megawatts each.

Since the 1980s, Karnataka has emerged as the pan-Indian leader in the field of IT (information technology). In 2007, there were nearly 2,000 firms operating in Karnataka. Many of them, including two of India's biggest software firms, Infosys and Wipro, are also headquartered in the state. Exports from these firms exceeded 50,000 crores ($12.5 billion) in 2006–07, accounting for nearly 38% of all IT exports from India. The Nandi Hills area in the outskirts of Devanahalli is the site of the upcoming $22 billion, 50 square kilometre BIAL IT Investment Region, one of the largest infrastructure projects in the history of Karnataka. All this has earned the state capital, Bangalore, the sobriquet *Silicon Valley of India.*

Karnataka also leads the nation in biotechnology. It is home to India's largest biocluster, with 158 of the country's 320 biotechnology firms being based here. The state accounts for 75% of India's floriculture, an upcoming industry which supplies flowers and ornamental plants worldwide.

Seven of India's banks, Canara Bank, Syndicate Bank, Corporation Bank, Vijaya Bank, Karnataka Bank, ING Vysya Bank and the State Bank of Mysore originated in this state.The coastal districts of Udupi and Dakshina Kannada have a branch for every 500 persons—the best distribution of banks in India. In March 2002, Karnataka had 4767 branches of different banks with each branch serving 11,000 persons, which is lower than the national average of 16,000.

A majority of the silk industry in India is headquartered in

Karnataka, much of it in Doddaballapura, and the state government intends to invest 70 crore in a "Silk City" at Muddenahalli, near Bangalore International Airport.

Economy of Karnataka

Karnataka is one of the highest economic growth states in India with an expected GSDP (Gross State Domestic Product) growth of 8.2% in the fiscal year 2010–2011. The total expected GSDP of Karnataka in 2010–2011 is about Rs.2719.56 billion. Per capita GSDP during 2008–2009 was US$1034.9. Karnataka recorded the highest growth rates in terms of GDP and per capita GDP in the last decade compared to other states. In 2008–09, the tertiary sector contributed the most to GSDP (US$31.6 billion%55 percent), followed by the secondary sector ($17 billion%29 percent), and the primary sector (US$9.5 billion%16 percent).

With an overall GDP growth of 56.2% and a per capita GDP growth of 43.9% in the last decade, Karnataka surpassed all other states in India, pushing Karnataka's per capita income in Indian Rupee terms to sixth place. Karnataka received US$2,026.4 million worth of Foreign Direct Investment for the fiscal year 2008–09, placing it at the third spot among states in India. At the end of 2004, the unemployment rate of Karnataka was 4.57% compared to a national rate of 5.99%. For the fiscal year 2006–07 the inflation rate of Karnataka was 4.4%, which was less than the national average.

Between 2011-12 and 2017-18, the GSDP of the state grew at a Compound Annual Growth Rate (CAGR) of 13.11 per cent to reach Rs12.69 trillion (US$ 196.88 billion) and the net state domestic product (NSDP) grew at a CAGR of 12.83 per cent to reach Rs 11.45 trillion (US$ 177.68 billion).

A fiscal year in Karnataka begins on 1 April of the previous calendar year and ends on 31 March of the year with which it is numbered.

After Bangalore urban district, Dakshina Kannada (Mangalore) and Belgaum district contribute the second and third highest revenue to the state respectively.

Agriculture and Livestock

Haystack on stilts in paddy fields of Uttara Kannada district

Agriculture is the primary occupation of most of Karnataka's rural residents. A total of 123,100 km^2 of land is cultivated in Karnataka, constituting 25.3% of the total geographical area of the state. According to the 2001 census, farmers and agricultural labourers formed 56% of the workforce of Karnataka. Agriculture in Karnataka is heavily dependent on the southwest monsoon since the extent of arid land in the state is second only to Rajasthan. Only 26.5% of sown area (30,900 km^2) is subjected to irrigation. The state has three agricultural seasons – Kharif (April to September), Rabi (October to December) and Summer (January to March).

Given below is a table of 2015 national output share of select agricultural crops and allied segments in Karnataka based on 2011 prices

Segment	National Share %
Mulberry	98.7
Coffee	82.7
Safflower	62.1

Ragi	59.2
Arecanut	58.6
Sunflower	55.2
Tamarind	32.4
Sericulture and Apiculture	28.9
Jowar	26.9
Horsegram	25.6
Sapota	24.6
Capsicum	19.9
Pomegranate	19.8
Water melon	19.7
Coconut	17.3
Grape	17.3
Floriculture	16.8
Narcotics	15.9
Wool and hair	14.8
Maize	14.5
Pepper	14.2
Cucumber	13.9
Condiments and spices	13.5
Sugarcane	10.7
Cashew nut	9.6
Arhar	9.4
Tobacco leaf	9.2
Tobacco stem	9.2
Fuel wood	8.4
Carrot	7.9
Tomato	7.2
Pineapple	7.1
Egg	6.7
Bean	6.6
Lemon	6.6
Pulse	6.5
Jackfruit	6.4
Turmeric	5.8
Cocoa	5.6

Groundnut	5.6
Marine fish	5.5
Ginger	5.4
Mango	5.4
Grass	5.2
Papaya	5.2
Rubber	5.1
Kitchen garden	5.0

Primary Crops grown in Karnataka

The main crops grown are Rice, Ragi, Jowar (sorghum), maize, and pulses (Tur and gram) in addition to oilseeds and a number of other cash crops. Cashews, coconut, arecanut, cardamom, chillies, cotton, sugarcane and tobacco are also produced. Karnataka is the largest producer of coarse cereals, coffee, raw silk and tomatoes among the states in India. Horticultural crops are grown in an area of 16,300 km^2 and the annual production is about 9.58 million tons. The income generated from horticulture constitutes over 40% of income generated from agriculture and it is about 17% of the state's GDP. In floriculture, Karnataka occupies the second position in India in terms of production and 700 tons of flowers (worth Rs.500 million) were produced in 2004–05.

Traditional Farming Methods are still in use

A majority of the thirty-five billion rupee silk industry in India is headquartered in Karnataka State, primarily in Mysore and North Bangalore regions of Doddaballapura, the site of a planned 700 million "Silk City".

Education

Karnataka is one the largest concentrations of higher education including medical and engineering colleges. Apart from Bengaluru, places like Mangalore, Belagavi, Mysuru, Hubballi-Dharwad and Davanagere have been producing professionals for the Information Technology industry. Muddenahalli, in North Bangalore, is the site of the upcoming Sri Sathya Sai Baba University and College of Medicine and a branch of the Visvesvaraya Institute of Advanced Technology. Devanahalli is set to be the location of a 95 billion Devanahalli Business Parks, which will contain Aerospace Education Special Economic Zones, near the Bengaluru International Airport. The North Bangalore region is set to be a premier educational hub of Karnataka.Dharwad in the northern part of the state is another hub for education with several engineering colleges and a central university. These developments are set to contribute significantly to Karnataka's economy by creating jobs, expanding educational opportunities, and spurring infrastructure development.

INDUSTRY

Karnataka evolved as the manufacturing hub for some of the largest public sector industries of India after India's independence. Hindustan Aeronautics Limited which is dedicated to research and development activities for indigenous fighter aircraft for the Indian Air Force employs over 9,500 employees making it one of the largest public sector employers in Karnataka.

Other heavy industries such as National Aerospace Laboratories, Bharat Heavy Electricals Limited, Indian Telephone Industries, Bharat Earth Movers Limited (BEML), Bharat Electronics Limited, Hindustan Machine Tools and Indian subsidiaries of Volvo and Toyota are also headquartered in Bangalore. India's national space agency, the Indian Space

Research Organization (ISRO), is headquartered in Bangalore and employs approximately 20,000 people.

TVS Motors has a motorcycle manufacturing plant at Mysore and Tata Motors at Dharwad. Karnataka state has many companies engaged in the manufacturing of electrical equipment and machinery like Kirloskar, ABB, Kavika, Larsen and Toubro etc. This may be due to the location of the Central Power Research Institute (CPRI) at Bangalore. Many multinational companies have set up their manufacturing units in Karnataka such as BASF, and Bosch.

The state owns sugar factories in the northern region, edible oil processing factories, pharmaceutical factories, textile processing centers, and steel producing facilities. Vishwesharaiya steel plant at Bhadravati is run by SAIL.

Minerals

Gold, iron ore, quartz, limestone, manganese, kyanite and bauxite are some of the minerals that are found in Karnataka. After the closure of the Kolar Gold Fields mine, the only company in India that produces gold by mining and extracting it from the ore is Hutti Gold Mines Limited that has plants at Hutti and Chitradurga in Karnataka. The major mines of manganese and iron ore are located at Sandur in Bellary district. Visweswaraiah Iron and Steel Ltd. at Bhadravathi and Jindal Vijayanagar Steel Ltd. at Toranagal are engaged in the production of iron and steel. Indian Aluminium Company Ltd (Hindalco) has an aluminum plant near Belgaum. Mysore Minerals Limited is in the mining and production of chromite industry in Hassan district. Rajashree Cements at Adityanagar, Vasavadatta Cements at Sedam and The Associated Cement Company Ltd. at Wadi are engaged in the production of cement. Uranium deposits have been found in Deshnur, a small village near Belgaum.

INFRASTRUCTURE

Physical infrastructure – roads

The state is well connected to its six neighboring states and other parts of India through 14 National Highways (NH); it accounts for about six percent of the total NH network in India. Its district centers are linked through 114 State Highways (SH). The total road network of NH, SH, and district roads is about 2,07,379 km, of which 1,27,541 km is surfaced (61.5 percent)

Road Type Road length (km)

National highways: 4,396

State highways: 28,311

District roads: 19,801

Physical infrastructure – airports

Domestic airports: Belgaum Airport, Mysore Airport and Hubli Airport

The curbside at Bangalore airport

International airports

Kempegowda International Airport, Devanahalli

Commissioned: May 2008

Area: 4,050 acres (16.4 km^2).

Capacity: 11 million paxp.a.

Aircraft Movements: 63,500

Third busiest airport in India (after Mumbai and Delhi).

Mangalore International Airport, Bajpe

Commissioned: December 1951

Passenger movements: 1,302,561

Aircraft movements: 11,861

Runways: 5300 ft. (Asphalt) and 8,038 ft. (concrete).

The only airport in Karnataka with two runways.

Physical infrastructure – ports

New Mangalore Port (2010–11).

Total traffic handled: 67.30 MTA.

Total imports handled: 23.6 MTA.

Total exports handled: 32.9 MTA.

Number of vessels: 1,186

Cruise vessels: 26

Revenue: US$65 million

KarwarPort (2007–08)

Total cargo handled: 2.7 MTA

Total imports and exports: 6 MTA

Revenue: US$2.7 million

25 Private liquid cargo tanks: 75,000 MT

Physical infrastructure – railways

Railway network of 3,172 km

Urban transport

Metro rail and mono-rail projects are underway in Bangalore. The first phase of the Namma Metro will cover a total of 42.3 km

Ongoing projects

Hassan–Sakhleshpura–Mangalore line gauge conversion is completed. Both freight and passenger trains run on this route on a daily basis connecting the seaport city of Mangaluru to the state capital of Bengaluru and Mysooru.

Key connectivity projects, doubling of Mysore–Bangalore railway line, Gadag–Bagalokot, Bangalore–Hassan to be taken up in the near future.

Physical infrastructure – power

Generation: Karnataka Power Corporation Limited and IPPs (GMR/Jindal/ Bhoruka)

KPCL has an installed capacity of over 9315 MW.

Number of consumers: 16.3 million

Independent power producers have installed capacity of 2,005 MW.

- KPCL -Karnataka Power Corporation Ltd.
- IPPs is Independent Power Producers

Transmission: Karnataka Power Transmission Corporation Limited (KPTCL).

Area covered: 192,000 km^2.

Sub stations: 1,205

Transmission lines: 28,000 km,33 kV, 130,000 km of 11 kV.

LT lines: 451855 km

Distribution transformers: 1,50,000

Physical infrastructure – power

Distribution/supply: Electricity Supply Companies (ESCOMs)

Bangalore Electricity Supply Company (BESCOM)

Mangalore Electricity Supply Company (MESCOM)

HubliElectricity Supply Company (HESCOM)

Gulbarga Electric Supply Company (GESCOM)

ChamundeshwariElectric Supply Corporation (CESC)

Physical infrastructure – telecommunications

Leading telecom companies in the sectors of telecommunication network, basic telephony services (both wire line and wireless) and networking services for telecommunication equipment are operating in the state. The entire State is networked via Optic FibreCables (OFC) by the state-run BSNL (formerly DOT) as well as private companies like Bharti, Reliance, VSNL and TATA Tele Services.

Last Mile Access is provided by BSNL as well as TATA Tele Services in various parts of the state. Bhartiand Reliance Communications provide the Last Mile Access directly to the customer in all major cities in Karnataka.

Seven new telephone exchanges were opened in 2007–2008.

Active telecom service providers in Karnataka.

BSNL, BhartiAirtel, Reliance Communications,Vodafone Essar, Spice Communications,Tata Teleservices Ltd.

Key statistics (2007–08)

Cellular subscribers : About 10 million

Internet/broadband

Subscribers: About 0.8 million

Telecom towers: About 14,000

Post offices: 9,826

Telephone connections provided: 2,610

Telephone exchanges: 2,727

Industrial infrastructure

Karnataka Industrial Area Development Board (KIADB) and Karnataka State Industrial Investment Development Corporation (KSIIDC) are jointly responsible for the development of industrial infrastructure in the state.

Directorate of Commerce and Industries has set up a district and taluk industrial centres across the state to facilitate investment

The Government of Karnataka is promoting the development of several SEZs across Karnataka such as pharma and biotech SEZ, food processing and agro-based industries and textiles SEZ at Hassan and IT and Coastal SEZs at Mangalore.

SOFTWARE INDUSTRY IN KARNATAKA

The software industry in Karnataka state in India has become one of the main pillars of economy. Karnataka stands first among all the states of India in terms of revenue generated from software exports. Software exports from Karnataka amounted to excess of 487 billion ($11.6 billion) in the year 2006-2007. This achievement has earned Karnataka's capital city Bangalore the sobriquet of *Silicon Valley of India.* This is because of the presence of major software companies in Bangalore and the revenue generated by exports of computer software. Though most software companies are located in Bangalore, some have settled in other cities like Mysore, Mangalore and Hubli in Karnataka. The Nandi Hills area in Devanahalli outskirts is the site of the upcoming $22 Billion, 12,000-acre (49 km^2) BIAL IT Investment Region, one of the largest infrastructure projects in the history of Karnataka. This edeavor expected to create four million jobs over by the year 2030. The infrastructure required for setting up software industries in Karnataka is provided by STPI. The software industry in Karnataka includes companies dealing with various fields like telecommunication, banking software, avionics, database, automotive, networking, semiconductors, mobile handsets, internet applications and business process outsourcing.

Origin

Starting in the 1980s, Karnataka emerged as the information technology capital of the country. A total of 1973 companies in Karnataka are involved in Information Technology related business including big firms like Infosys and Wipro who have their headquarters in Bangalore. The origin of the growth of the software industry in Karnataka seems to have been the entry of Texas Instruments which was the first multinational to set up base in Sona Tower, Millers Road, Bangalore in 1985.Texas Instruments was searching for a location to set up their overseas development centre in India in the early 1980s. They first looked at the states of Maharashtra and Tamil Nadu but when both states refused permission, Karnataka was approached with a condition that land allotted must be near an airport. The then chief minister of Karnataka Gundu Rao agreed to their terms and granted land near the HAL Airport in Bangalore. Texas Instruments currently has a big facility in Bagmane Tech Park in Bangalore near the airport.

There were many factors conducive to the development of the software industry in Karnataka state. One factor is the presence of large numbers of top grade science and engineering institutions like IISc, NITK, B.M.S. College of Engineering, BVB, Malnad College of Engineering MSRIT, NIE, SJCE, RVCE, PESIT, SDMCET and around 200 engineering colleges. The software industry requires large numbers of skilled engineers which are regularly churned out of the engineering colleges in Karnataka. The presence of Public sector undertakings like BEL, HAL, BHEL, ITI and BEML gave ready access to manpower as well as trial opportunities of newly developed software. There were many advanced laboratories like NAL and ISRO in and around Bangalore which provided necessary basic knowledge required for software development. The successive state governments have been proactive in providing necessary facilities for growth of the industry. The salubrious climate of Bangalore also helps in the growth of the software industry there.

Effects

There has been both positive and negative effects of software industry's tremendous growth. The per capita income of state has risen. The software engineers of the current generation earn salaries at the beginning of their career more than what their parents used to earn at the end of their career. This affluence can be seen with young engineers flaunting new electronic gadgets. Cars once considered a luxury has become a commodity, often leading to traffic jams and unavailability of space for parking. More people are traveling abroad for work as well as for tourism. Growth in income has had an effect on the real estate prices with the land rates skyrocketing. Land prices have shot much beyond rate of inflation and in some places rate of land doubles every two years. Agriculture has slowed down as people find it more lucrative to sell the land rather than use it for agriculture. The surge in income of software professionals has led to increased interest among youth opting for computer science and information technology courses in college. The basic science, arts and commerce fields have felt a shortage of quality manpower. The current global recession of economy has hit software industry with some losing their jobs.

ECONOMY OF BANGALORE

The Economy of Bangalore is an important part of the economy of India as a whole and contributes over 87% to the Economy of the State of Karnataka, accounting for 98% of the Software Exports of the State.

The headquarters of Infosys, India's second largest IT company, is located in Bangalore

The establishment and success of high technology firms in Bangalore has led to the growth of Information Technology (IT) in India. IT firms in Bangalore employ about 35% of India's pool of 2.5 million IT professionals and account for the highest IT-related exports in the country.

Estimates of the city's Metro GDP are around 110 billion USD, and it has been ranked as either fourth- or fifth-most productive metro area of India.

The Public Utilities Building is a major economic center

One of the important factors spurring Bangalore's growth was heavy central government investment in Bangalore's public sector industries, partially because it is geographically out-of-reach from India's rivals Pakistan and China. This led to the concentration of technical and scientific navigator in Bangalore, and is a factor in leading the "IT revolution" in Bangalore. Karnataka's political leaders such as D. Devaraj Urs, Ramakrishna Hegde, Gundu Rao, Veerappa Moily, H.D.Deve Gowda, J. H. Patel and S.M. Krishna each played a pivotal role in the development of Information Technology and Business Process Outsourcing (BPO) in Bangalore. When R. K. Baliga, Founder of the Electronics City proposed the concept of developing the electronic city in the early 1970s it was met with skepticism but Chief Minister D. Devaraj Urs at that time supported him and approved the project. This initial seed investment by the Karnataka State Government in 1976 laid the foundation for the Electronics City.

Startups

Further meriting its nickname of the Silicon Valley of India, Bengaluru is home to India's largest start-ups (Flipkart, Ola Cabs, iD Fresh Foods) and has been repeatedly recognised as and rated the best city in India and one of the best in the world to start your own company.

Complimented by the booming IT industry and venture capitalists and investors such as Goldman Sachs and NASDAQ, whose India branches are based out of Bengaluru, make it the perfect place for new tech companies.

Bengaluru is also home to the majority of India's unicorns and to the world's largest pure-play data analytics firm - Mu Sigma. The Koramangala neighbourhood has one of the highest densities of start-ups in the world, second only to Silicon Valley, California.

Aerospace and Aviation industries

Bangalore also called the aviation monopoly capital of India. It accounts India's more than 65% aerospace business. World Aerospace giants such as Boeing, Airbus, Goodrich, Dynamatics, Honeywell, GE Aviation, UTL, others have their R&D and Engineering centres.

Long before Bangalore was called the Silicon Valley of India, the city made its name as headquarters to some of the largest public sector heavy industries of India. The Hindustan Aeronautics Limited (HAL) headquarters is in Bangalore, and is dedicated to research and development activities for indigenous fighter aircraft for the Indian Air Force. With over 9,500 employees, it is one of the largest public sectoremployers in Bangalore.

The Sukhoi-30MKI is a dual-role fighter that is manufactured under license of Sukhoi by Bangalore-based Hindustan Aeronautics Limited for the Indian Air Force.

Today, HAL manufactures, under license, various fighter aircraft for the Indian Air Force (IAF) including Sukhoi 30 Flankers and Jaguars. HAL also develops indigenous products for the IAF such as HAL Tejas, Aeronautical Development Agency, HAL Dhruv and HAL HF-24 Marut.

The National Aerospace Laboratories (NAL) is also headquartered in Bangalore and is dedicated to the development of civil aviation technologies. Incorporated in 1960, NAL often works in conjunction with the HAL and has a staff strength of over 1,300 employees. NAL also investigates aircraft malfeasance.

A 1,000-acre (4.0 km^2) special economic zone for the aerospace industry is being set up near the Bangalore International Airport. Bangalore was also home to large domestic airlines - now defunct Simplifly Deccan and Kingfisher Airlines.

Manufacturing Industries

Other heavy industries in Bangalore include Bharat Electronics Limited, Bharat Heavy Electricals Limited (BHEL),

Indian Telephone Industries (ITI), Bharat Earth Movers Limited (BEML), HMT (formerly Hindustan Machine Tools), Hindustan Motors (HM) and ABB Group.

Bangalore is also becoming a destination for the automotive industry. Volvo has a manufacturing plant in Bangalore.

Bangalore houses many small and medium scale industries in its Peenya industrial area that claimed to be one of the biggest in Asia 30-years ago; newly including Apple's India manufacturing plant - the only active plant outside of China.

Space technology

In June 1972, the Government of India set up the Space Commission and Department of Space (DOS). India's premier space research organization, the ISRO was created under the DOS and headquartered in Bangalore. The main objective of ISRO includes development of satellites and launch vehicles. Aryabhata, India's first satellite, was developed and successfully launched by ISRO. Since then, the organization has successfully launched numerous other satellites such as Bhaskara, Rohini, APPLE, and the INSAT series, and successfully deployed PSLVs and GSLVs. ISRO also heads India's ambitious moon and Mars program.

Biotechnology

Biotechnology is a rapidly expanding field in the city. Bangalore accounts for at least 97 of the approximately 240 biotechnology companies in India. Interest in Bangalore as a base for biotechnology companies stems from Karnataka's comprehensive biotechnology policy, described by the Karnataka Vision Group on Biotechnology. In 2003-2004, Karnataka attracted the maximum venture capital funding for biotechnology in the country - $8 million. Biocon, headquartered in Bangalore, is the nation's leading biotechnology company and ranks 16th in the world in revenues.

Institute of Bioinformatics and Applied Biotechnology (IBAB), initiated by Biotechnology vision group, ICICI and Biocon (located at ITPL) is trying to shape revolutionary scientists in the field.

Like the software industry which initially drew most of its workforce from the local public sector engineering industries, the biotechnology industry had access to talent from the National Center of Biological Sciences (NCBS) and the Indian Institute of Science (IISc).

Biocon, headquartered in Bangalore, is one of India's largest biotechnology companies.

And Indian Biotechnology Research Organisation (IBRO) is recently under process of development to boost Biotechnology Growth in India, providing the Advanced Research and Talent pool to India from IBRO, whose mission and vision is Research and Development in Biotechnology to make India as a Global Leader in Biotechnology.

Other Major Biotechnology company based out of Bangalore is Advanta India.

TRANSPORT IN KARNATAKA

Karnataka, a state in South India has a well-developed transport system. Its capital city, Bengaluru is well-connected by air to domestic and international destinations and the Kempegowda International Airport (KIA) in the city is one of the busiest airports in India. It was also the headquarters of the airlines Air Deccan and Kingfisher Airlines. The road transport is also well developed in the state with many National and State highways providing means for fast transportation. The headquarters of the South-Western Railway division of Indian Railways is located at Hubballi and this division governs most of the railway network in the state. Konkan Railway which passes along the coastal region of the state is considered as one of the toughest engineering projects being undertaken in India till date. Buses, cars and trains are the means of transport for moving across distant places in Karnataka. For transportation within the city or town limits; motorbikes, cars, autorickshaws and buses are used. With the advent of low-cost airlines, many people are choosing to travel via air as well.

Air transport

Mangaluru and Bengaluru are the only two cities in the state that have International flights operating from their airports. Kempegowda International Airport is host to 9 domestic airlines and 19 international airlines and Lufthansa, British Airways, Air France, Singapore Airlines and Malaysia Airlines, connecting the city to almost 50 destinations across India and the world. With Bengaluru being the 'IT capital' of India, the air traffic to this city has increased manifold.

Mangalore International Airport on the other hand connects 7 international destinations which includes Dubai, Bahrain, Qatar, Dammam, Kuwait, Abu Dhabi, Muscat and domestic destinations like Mumbai, Delhi, Bengaluru, Calicut, Chennai. Mangalore International Airport has recorded 28.1% annual growth in passenger traffic for the year 2015-2016 by carrying 1.67 million passengers, making it the fastest growing airport in the state.

Hubli Airport (IATA: HBX, ICAO: VOHB) is one of the major operational airports serving northern Karnataka. Currently SpiceJet Airlines have started its operation from Hubli To Bangalore, Mumbai, Hyderabad, Jabalpur, Mangalore, Chennai And Indigo Airlines have started it's operation from Hubli to Ahmedabad, Chennai, Bangalore, Cochin, Goa, Alliance Air operates one flight everyday to the state capital Bangalore,

Air India has started its operation from Hubli to Mumbai and Bangalore on Tuesday, Wednesday and Saturday. and Star Air (India) will start its operation Hubli To Bangalore, Delhi (Hindon), Pune, and Tirupati on September 15 The airport is currently being upgraded to an international airport.

Mysore Airport Many airlines disconnected the service from mysore as flights which plied to Kempegowda International airport did not go well. New routes of air service were introduced under the UDAAN scheme to hyderabad and chennai everyday which received great response.

Additional to that the state operates flights from bangalore to mysore during dasara festival. The airport landed in major controversies with the runway expansion. A decision was taken to build an underpass as it was blocked by rail route and and a national highway connecting Kozhikode - a first kind in the country.

Plans are to develop this major tourist destination's airport to an international service as there is competition now from the upcoming Kannur International Airport.

Belgaum Airport is the Oldest Airport in North Karnataka, Alliance Air(India) operate To Bangalore thrice a week Tue, wed, sat, Air India started operation to Bangalore four days a week Mon, thu, fri, Sun.

there are airports at Bellary Airport and Bidar Airport that do not have any air service. In addition, there are private airstrips at Sedam Airport, Koppal Airport and Harihar Airport.

Hassan Airport, Karnataka, Kalaburagi Airport, Bijapur Airport and Shivamogga Airport, built under the Public Private Partnership (PPP) model, was opened for commercial use by July 2013.

Rail transport

The total length of rail track in Karnataka is 3089 km For a long time after independence, the railway network in the state was under the Southern and Western railway zones which were headquartered at Chennai and Mumbai respectively. The South Western Zone, headquartered at Hubballi was created in 2003 thus fulfilling a long-standing demand of the state. Several parts of the state now come under this zone with the remaining being under Southern Railways. Coastal Karnataka is covered under the Konkan railway network, a project that is regarded as one of the feats of Indian engineering and included the construction of a bridge of length 2,023 metres (6,637 ft) across the river Sharavathi at Honnavar and a tunnel of length 2,960 metres (9,711 ft) at Karwar. Bengaluru, the capital city, is extensively connected with inter-state destinations while other important cities and towns in the state are not so well-connected.The train connectivity within Karnataka has improved since K.H.Muniyappa, Member of Parliament from Kolar constituency has been the Union Minister of State for Railways.

- Mangaluru, one of the major cities in Karnataka now has a train service to other major cities like Bengaluru, Mysuru started on 8 December 2007, but not directly to Hubballi. There is a proposed railway line between Hubballi and Ankola to fulfill this demand.
- Shivamogga-Talaguppa, Mysore-Chamarajanagar meter-gauge tracks has been converted to broad-gauge. There is a direct train service from Mysuru to Talaguppa which is very close to the world-famous Jog Falls.An announcement regarding the extension of Bangalore-Shivamogga Express (night train) to Talaguppa has been made in the Railway Budget 2012-13. There are 4 direct passenger trains running from Mysuru to Chamarajanagar and a Chamarajanagar-Tirupati fast passenger which connects to the state capital Bengaluru via Mysuru.
- District capital like Madikeri is not connected by a rail network.A rail link to Madikeri would be difficult since it is a hill station and any construction activity would harm the pristine environment.
- The district of Kodagu has no railway track within it.However a survey is under progress to link Mysuru with Kushalnagar in Kodagudistrict.

- Doubling of the track between Bengaluru and Mysuru (a line that receives very good patronage) is already completed.
- Though the state has Konkan Railway within it; it has remained isolated with no trains running from other parts of the state to places that exist on the Konkan Railway.

The superfast Shatabdi Express trains run from Bengaluru to Chennai and Mysuru. A *Jan Shatabdi* express runs from Bengaluru to Hubballiand this is the first train in India that has been fitted with a GPS (Global Position System) based Location Announcement System. Using this system, the passengers are announced apriori the arrival of a station. Konkan Railway is an engineering marvel; the construction of which included the bridge across the river Sharavathi at Honnavar of length 2,023 m and a tunnel at Karwar of length 2,960 m.

A high-end luxury train operated by the Tourism Department of Karnataka The Golden Chariot covers the places of interest in Karnataka and Goa under the tour name "Pride of the South". Places Covered: Bengaluru - Kabini/Bandipur - Mysuru - Hassan - Hampi - Gadag - Goa - Bengaluru. The same train covers the places of interest in Karnataka, Tamil Nadu, Kerala with a different tour name "Southern Splendour". Places Covered: Bengaluru - Chennai - Mamallapuram - Pondicherry - Tiruchirapalli & Thanjavur - Madurai - Kanyakumari - Thiruvananthapuram - Backwaters & Kochi / Allepey - Bengaluru.

Water transport

Karnataka has 1 major port; the New Mangaluru Port and 10 minor ports; Karwar, Belekeri, Tadri, Honnavara, Bhatkal, Kundapur, Hangarkatta, Malpe, Padubidri and Old Mangaluru. The construction of the New Mangaluru Port was started in 1962 and completed in 1974. It was incorporated as the 9th major port in India on 4 May 1974. This port handled 32.04 million tonnes of traffic in the fiscal year 2006-07 with 17.92

million tonnes of imports and 14.12 million tonnes of exports. This was actually a slowdown in traffic at this port compared to the previous fiscal year mainly due to the reduction in iron ore exports from the Kudremukha Iron Ore Company limited. The port also handled 1015 vessels including 18 cruise vessels during the year 2006-07. The sector of Inland water transport within the rivers of Karnataka is not well-developed.

Road transport

Among the network of roads in Karnataka, 3973 km. of roads are National Highways. Karnataka also has state highways of length 9829 km.

The public bus transport in Karnataka is managed by the Karnataka State Road Transport Corporation (KSRTC). It was set up in 1961 with the objective of providing adequate, efficient, economic and properly coordinated road transport services. It operates 5100 schedules using 5400 vehicles covering 1.95 million kilometres and an average of 2.2 million passengers daily. About 25000 people are employed in KSRTC. For better management of public transport, KSRTC was bifurcated into three Corporations viz., Bangalore Metropolitan Transport Corporation, Bengaluru on 15 August 1997, North-west Karnataka Road Transport Corporation, Hubballi on 1 November 1997 and North-East Karnataka Road Transport Corporation, Gulbarga on 1st Oct 2000. The reservation system is networked and computerised and tickets can be availed at designated kiosks in towns and cities. An online reservation system called *AWATAR* has also been devised by KSRTC using which travellers can reserve tickets online. KSRTC plies various categories of buses viz. Airavat Club-Class (high-end luxury Volvo, Scania, Mercedes-Benz multi-axle AC buses), Airavat (high-end luxury Volvo and Mercedes Benz AC buses), Ambaari(Corona AC and non AC Sleeper buses), Rajahamsa Executive (Deluxe buses built on Leyland, Eicher and Tata chassis), Karnataka Vaibhav (Semi-Deluxe buses built on Leyland, Eicher and Tata chassis), Karnataka Saarige (Bus service linking rural areas to major settlements as well as the cheapest alternative for inter-city or town routes. The buses are built on Tata and Leyland chassis). *Grameena Sarige* is another initiative by KSRTC to provide bus service to the rural populace of the state.

Buses run by private persons are allowed to operate in few districts of Karnataka.Inter district transportation are run by private operators, connecting capital Bengaluru and main cities like Mangaluru and Dharwad to district headquarters. Intra district transportation by private operators is currently allowed in Dakshina Kannada and Udupi districts. Omni bus and Maxi cabs are also other modes of road transportation in the state, especially where KSRTC does not buses or run very few.

7

Tourism

TOURISM

By virtue of its varied geography and long history, Karnataka hosts numerous spots of interest for tourists. There is an array of ancient sculptured temples, modern cities, scenic hill ranges, forests and beaches.

Karnataka has been ranked as the fourth most popular destination for tourism among the states of India. Karnataka has the second highest number of nationally protected monuments in India, second only to Uttar Pradesh, in addition to 752 monuments protected by the State Directorate of Archaeology and Museums. Another 25,000 monuments are yet to receive protection.

Keshava Temple, Somanathapura

Gol Gumbaz at Bijapur, has the second largest pre-modern dome in the world after the Byzantine Hagia Sophia.

The districts of the Western Ghats and the southern districts of the state have popular eco-tourism locations including Kudremukh, Madikeri and Agumbe. Karnataka has 25 wildlife sanctuaries and five national parks. Popular among them are Bandipur National Park, Bannerghatta National Park and Nagarhole National Park.

Mysore Palace at night, Mysore

The ruins of the Vijayanagara Empire at Hampi and the monuments of Pattadakal are on the list of UNESCO's World Heritage Sites. The cave temples at Badami and the rock-cut temples at Aihole representing the Badami Chalukyan style of architecture are also popular tourist destinations. The Hoysala temples at Belur and Halebidu, which were built with Chloritic schist (soapstone) are proposed UNESCO World Heritage sites.The Gol Gumbaz and Ibrahim Rauza are famous examples of the Deccan Sultanate style of architecture. The monolith of Gomateshwara Bahubali at Shravanabelagola is the tallest sculpted monolith in the world, attracting tens of thousands of pilgrims during the Mahamastakabhisheka festival.

Mysore painting depicting Goddess Saraswati

The waterfalls of Karnataka and Kudremukh are considered by some to be among the "1001 Natural Wonders of the World". Jog Falls is India's tallest single-tiered waterfall with Gokak Falls, Unchalli Falls, Magod Falls, Abbey Falls and Shivanasamudra Falls among other popular waterfalls.

Several popular beaches dot the coastline, including Murudeshwara, Gokarna, Malpe and Karwar. In addition, Karnataka is home to several places of religious importance. Several Hindu temples including the famous Udupi Sri Krishna Matha, the Marikamba Temple at Sirsi, the Kollur Mookambika Temple, the Sri Manjunatha Temple at Dharmasthala, Kukke Subramanya Temple and Sharadamba Temple at Shringeri attract pilgrims from all over India. Most of the holy sites of Lingayatism, like Kudalasangama and Basavana Bagewadi, are found in northern parts of the state. Shravanabelagola, Mudabidri and Karkala are famous for Jain history and monuments. Jainism had a stronghold in Karnataka in the early medieval period with Shravanabelagola as its most important centre. The Shettihalli Rosary Church near Shettihalli, an example of French colonial Gothic architecture, is a rare example of a Christian ruin, is a popular tourist site.

Recently Karnataka has emerged as a center of health care tourism. Karnataka has the highest number of approved health systems and alternative therapies in India. Along with some ISO certified government-owned hospitals, private institutions which provide international-quality services have caused the health care industry to grow by 30% during 2004–05. Hospitals in Karnataka treat around 8,000 health tourists every year.

TOURISM PLACE IN KARNATAKA

Mahamastakabhisheka of Gommateshwara statue (the largest ancient monolithic statue in the world), at Shravanabelagola

Virupaksha Temple Hampi

Karnataka, the eighth largest state in India, has been ranked as the third most popular state in the country for tourism in 2014. It is home to 507 of the 3600 centrally protected monuments in India, the largest number after Uttar Pradesh. The State Directorate of Archaeology and Museums protects an additional 752 monuments and another 25,000 monuments are yet to receive protection. Tourism centres on the ancient sculptured temples, modern cities, the hill ranges, forests and beaches. Broadly, *tourism in Karnataka* can be divided into four geographical regions: North Karnataka, the Hill Stations, Coastal Karnataka and South Karnataka.

The Karnataka government has recently introduced The Golden Chariot – a train which connects popular tourist destinations in the state and Goa.

North Karnataka

North Karnataka has monuments that date back to the 5th century. Kannada empires that ruled the Deccan had their capitals here. Badami Chalukyas monuments are located at Pattadakal, Aihole and Badami. Aihole has been called *the cradle of Indian architecture* and has over 125 temples and monuments built between 450 and 1100 BC. Rashtrakuta monuments at Lokapura, Bilgi and Kuknur and Kalyani Chalukyas monuments built in *Gadag style of architecture* at

Lakkundi, Gadag, Itagi (in Koppal District) and the Vijayanagar empire temples at Vijayanagaraare some examples. Hampi in Bellary District has ruins spread over an area of 125 km^2. With some fifty four world heritage monuments and six hundred and fifty national monuments (*ASI*). An additional three hundred monuments await protection. The Deccan sultanate monuments at Bijapur and Gulbarga show unique and discreet Hindu influences and rival the Muslim monuments of North India. Archeologically important locations like Sannati, Kanaganahalli in Gulbarga district have thrown more light on Buddhist centres of the 1st century BCE to 3rd century CE. The first ever statue of emperor Ashoka with his queens and a Prakrit inscription *Rayo Ashoka* (*ASI*) has been found.

Badami surroundings important locations are Kudalasangama, Aihole, Pattadakal, Mahakutaand Banashankari. Hampi surroundings region, they can be visited from Hampi/Hosapete, or from Hubli. There are Kuknur, Itagi, Gadag, Lakkundi, Dambal, Haveri, Kaginele, Bankapura.

World heritage centres

Mallikarjuna and Kasivisvanatha temples at Pattadakal

- Hampi, Bellary District: The site of the capital of Vijayanagara (1336) and formerly the seat of the Vijayanagar Empire. Foreign visitors in the 15th and 16th centuries described Hampi as being bigger than Rome. The city was destroyed and deserted in 1565 by marauding Moghul invaders and its ruins now lie scattered over a 26 sq. km area south of the river Tungabhadra. The rocky area near Anegundi to the north of the river has been identified as Kishkindha of Ramayana times. Hampi is home to a 29-foot-tall (8.8 m) monolithic Narasimha, which was installed by Krishnadevaraya in 1529. The remains of palaces and gateways can be seen.
- Group of 8th-century CE monuments, Pattadakal: Located on the banks of the river Malaprabha, Pattadakal was the second capital of the Chalukyas and contains examples of 7th- and 8th-century temple architecture. Four temples are in the south Indian Dravidian style, four in the North Indian *Nagara* style and the last one, the Papanatha temple represents a hybrid of the two styles. The oldest temples are the Sangameshwara, Mallikarjuna and Virupaksha Temples.

Historical locations

Western Chalukya

- Aihole: a former Chalukya trading city. There are around 140 temples including examples of early Chalukya, Rashtrakuta and later Chalukya dynasties from the 6th to 12th centuries. It has a Jain and Vedic rock-cut shrine, both of about the 6th century. It has Tirthankara images and a Durga temple. The meguti on a hill is a jaina basti which has an Aihole inscription of Pulakeshin 2 and also a Buddhist two-storied rock -cut shrine below it. All the other Jain and Buddhist temples are built of stone and resemble Hindu temples. The temples were built during the Middle Ages before any style was established and hence there is a mixture of styles.

- Badami: the capital of the early Chalukyas in the 6th century, is at the mouth of a ravine between two rocky hills. The town is known for its cave temples (all carved out of sandstone hills). Badami have four caves, the cave temple dedicated to Vishnu is the largest. In front of the cave temple, there is a reservoir called Aghastya Teertha dotted with temples on its bank. Among them, two are dedicated to Vishnu, one to Shiva and the fourth is a Jain Temple. Carvings in the cave temples display the Hindu gods, Narashima and Hari Hara. The temples also have paintings on the ceiling and bracket figures on the piers.

Cave temple 3 Badami

- Basavana Bagewadi: It is 43 east of Bijapur. In the 12th century, Saint Basaveshwara was born here. It was an agrahara. The main temple here is in the Chalukya style and it was called as Sangamantha in records. The Samadhis of Siddharameshwara and Gurupadeshwara of the Inchageri school of spiritual pursuit are seen here.
- Basavakalyana, Bidar District: former capital of the Later Chalukyas. It has an old fort renovated by the Bahamani containing an Archaeological Museum. Few Chalukya or Kalachuri remains exist except the Chalukya Narayanapur temple in the outskirts of the town. There is a modern Basaveshwara temple, Prabhudevara Gadduge, Jurist of the Kalyani Chalukyas period. Vijnaneshwara's Cave, Madivala Machiah's Pond, Akka Nagamma's Cave, fully renovated Siddheshwara temple and a new structure called Anubhava Mantapa, the Qaji's mosque and Raja Bagh Sawar Dargah.
- Annigeri (30 km from Hubli): It has an Amriteshwara temple of the time of the Kalyani Chalukyas. It was the birthplace of great Kannada Poet Pampa and there is a Jain basadi of Parshwanatha. It was once a headquarters of Belvola-300. It was the capital of ChalukyaSomeshwara 4. In addition to Veerashaiva Mathas; there is a ruined Banashankari Temple and seven mosques and also an ancient Veerabhadra temple.

Rashtrakuta dynasty

- Malkhed, Gulbarga District
- Naregal, Gadag District
- Belgaum Fort

Kadamba dynasty

- Halasi: The place is in Background of Western Ghats in lush, green atmosphere. It was the second capital of the Kadambas of Banavasi. The huge Bhuvaraha Narasimha temple has tall images of Varaha, Narasimha, Narayana and Surya. Halasi has a fort and temples of

Gokarneshswara, Kapileshwara, Swarneshwara and Hatakeshwara.

Large domical ceiling in the main hall at **Tarateshwara temple** *Hangal*

- Hangal: Hanagal was the capital of Hangal Kadambas, feudatories of Kalyani Chalukyas. It was mentioned as Panungal in records and identified by tradition with Viratanagara of Mahabharatha days. It is on the left bank of the Dharma River. The *Tarakeshwara temple* here is a huge structure with series of images and polished tall Chalukya pillars. The other temples are Virabhadra, Billeshwara and Ramalinga etc. There is a Veerashaiva Kumaraswamy Matha here.
- Banavasi: Banavasi was the capital of Kadambas. The place is on the bank of the Varada river and its laterite fort is surrounded by the river at its three sides. Ashoka

is said to have sent his missionaries to 'Vanavasa'. Banavasi also contains Buddhist brick monuments. Chutu prince Nagashri built a Buddhist Vihara, a tank and installed a Naga image at the place according to a Prakrit record at the place. There is also a monument at Banavasi, Mudhukeshvara temple and also Kadamba Nagara Shikhara is seen on the garbhagriha of this temple. Records here indicate that Buddhism and Jainism were popular.

Deccan Sultanates

Jumma Masjid at Lakshmeshwar, North Karnataka

- Bijapur: The former capital of the Adil Shahi Kings (1489–1686). Gol Gumbaz is the mausoleum of Muhammed Adil Shah and was built in 1659. It houses the world's second largest dome, unsupported by pillars. Malik-e-Maidan is a 55-ton cannon perched on a platform. The head of the cannon is fashioned into the shape of a lion whose jaws are trying to devour an elephant.
- Bidar: a centre for Bidriware. It is the location of the tombs of 30 rulers including the Chaukhandi of Hazrat Khalil-Ullah Shah and Sultan Ahmed Shah Al Wali Bahamani from the Bahamani dynasty.
- Gulbarga
- Raichur
- Lakshmeshwar: The Jumma Masjid, built during the rule of Adilshahi, has a large crowning onion dome and Koranic scripture written in gold.

Rattas

- Saundatti: The town proper has a fort on the hill built during the 17th century, by Sirasangi Desai, with eight bastions. It was the *capital of Rattas* who later shifted their headquarters to Belgaum. There are two temples of Ankeshwara, Puradeshwara, Mallikarjuna, Venkateshwara and the Veerabhadra. The Renukasagar waters touch the outskirts of Saundatti. Tourist attractions of this region are Hooli Panchalingeshwara temple, Renuka (Yallamma) temple, Saundatti Fort, Parasgad Fort, Navilateertha.

Places of worship

- Devala Ganagapura, It is the second incarnation of Lord Dattatreya away from Afzalpur taluk around 25 km, Gulbarga District: It is 651 km from Bangalore. Sri Narasimha Saraswati stayed here for a long time and was granted a jahgir by the Bahmani Sultan. The sultan believed that the saint had cured him of a large boil. The saint is treated by his followers as an incarnation of

Dattatreya. The Saint has cured the Sultan of a serious boil. The Saint is treated as an incarnation of Dattatreya and devotees from Maharashtra and Karnataka. It is a very holy place.

Shiva temples

Kudalasangama in Bagalkot district

Gokarna is a great all-India centre where the Atmalinga (Mahabaleshwara) of Shiva, brought by Ravana is believed to have been installed. Nearby is Murudeshwar where a huge modern Shiva temple in Dravidian Style has been raised, renovating an ancient shrine. Both the places are on the sea-shore in Uttara Kannada. At Hampi is the Virupaksha Temple, venerated by generations of poets, scholars, kings and commoners.

The Shiva temple at Kudalasangama in Bagalkot District is associated with Saint Basaveshwara. Equally remarkable pieces of art are the Virupaksha and the Mallikarjuna at Pattadakal in Bagalkote dt.

The Veerashaivas have many venerated places, either associated with Basaveshwara or his contemporaries. Basavana Bagewadi was his place of birth and Kudala Sangama the place of his spiritual practices, are in Bijapur and Bagalkot dts. The latter is at the confluence of the river Krishna and the Malaprabha. Basava Kalyana (Kalyani), the ancient Chalukya capital in Bidar District was the place where he conducted his socio-religious movement. Ulavi in Uttara Kannada, a quiet place amidst forests, has the samadhi of Chennabasavanna, Basaveshwara's nephew. Belgami (Balligavi), the Chalukya art centre in Shimoga dt. is identified as the birthplace of Allama Prabhu and Uduthadi near it, is the native place of Akka Mahadevi. Later Veerashaiva saints are associated with many places. Kodekal (Gulbarga dt.) Basavanna temple, Kadakola Madivallajja Matha, Sharana Basaveshwara temple and Dasoha Math at Gulbarga are few more places of worship.

Athani has the samadhi of the Veerashaiva Saint Shivayogi. Some of the outstanding Veerashaiva Mathas are seen at Naganur near Bailhongal and Kalmatha in Belgaum, Durudundeshwara Matha at Arabhavi and Mahantaswamy Matha at Murgod are in Belgaum dt. Murugha Matha (Dharwad), Annadaneshwara Matha (Mundargi), Tontadarya Matha at Gadag and Dambal, Moorusavira Matha at Hubli, Murugha Matha and Hukkeri Matha (Haveri), Taralabalu Matha at Sirigere, Murugharajendra Matha at Chitradurga, Banthanala Shivajogi Matha at Chadachan and Mahantaswamy Matha (Ilkal) are equally notable. The samadhi of Sharanabasappa Appa at Gulbarga.

Coastal Karnataka

Coastal Karnataka is the stronghold of Hindu and Jain pilgrimage spots with Udupi and its many temples being the centre of Dvaitaphilosophy, Gokarna is known for Vedic studies, Sringeri has the first of the Shankaracharya mathas and is important for its Advaitaphilosophy, Karkala and Mudabidri are well known places of Jain worship and Vaishnava rituals. Exquisite Vijayanagar temples built in Chalukya – Malabar region combinational style are seen in Bhatkal, Kumta, Shirali etc. The warm beaches of Karnataka are mostly unspoiled.

Jamboti, 20 km south-west of Belgaum, has popular evergreen hilltop forests.

Karnataka is blessed with over 300 km of pristine coastal stretch. Netrani Island of Uttara Kannada is known for coral reefs. St. Mary's Island, a few kilometres from Udupi has basalt rock formations. Sunny beaches at places like Malpe, Murdeshwara, Maravanthe, Gokarna, Kumta have spectacular mountains to the east. Agumbe, Kodachadri hills, Kemmangundi, are just a few of many hill stations that straddle the coast providing tourists sun and greenery. Unlike many crowded hill stations in South India, the hill stations of Karnataka are still mostly undiscovered and pristine.

- Gokarna: The Coastal town of Gokarna is a pilgrimage centre as well as a centre of Sanskrit learning, 56 km from Karwar. It has the Mahabaleswar Temple with the 'Atmalinga' dedicated to Shiva. There is an enormous chariot, which is taken out in a procession on Shiva's birthday in February. The Tambraparni Teertha here is considered sacred to perform obsequies of the dead. There is a beach called *Om Beach.*
- Udupi: One of the holy place and it is 58 km from Mangalore. The Krishna temple here is founded by Acharya Madhwa during the 14th century. He founded eight mathas to conduct the services of Lord Krishna in turns. Paryaya festival is held once in two years in January. The place has Kadiyali Durga temple, Ambalapadi Shakti temple, Raghavendra Matha and the Venkataraman swamy temple. Malpe is the port near here. It has a beach and the Vadabhandeshwara temple of Balarama.
- Thantrady : One of the holy place and it is 22 km from Udupi. The brammasthana temple here founded by sri Ramanna bairy. It was an astabanda bramha. The main archaka of this temple is Nagaraj bairy.
- Karkala: 50 km from Mangalore and 20 km from North of Moodabidire, is Karkala, an important centre of Jainism. There are several temples and a 17 metres high statue

of Bahubali (Gomateshwara), situated on a small hill. The statue is a naked figure reached by a flight of rock-cut steps. Some of the temples are Chaturmukha Basti (1587), Neminatha Basti, Ananthapadmanabha Temple (1567) dedicated to Vishnu, and Venkataramana temple (Padutirupathi).

- Venur: Situated 50 km NE of Mangalore, has eight Bastis and ruins of a Mahadeva temple. The largest of them is the 17C Kalli Basti, dedicated to Shantinatha. There is a Gommateshwara Monolith, 11metres high dating back to 1604 in Venur.
- Malpe Beach: Situated 66 km north of Mangalore, near Manipal. It has a tourist beach. The uninhibited St. Mary's Island, accessible by boat, has a beach and an impressive geological formation of basalt rock pillars into the sea.
- Dharmastala: Situated 75 km from Mangalore, Dharmastala is an attractive site surrounded by forested hills, rice fields and by the river Netravati on all sides. The Manjunatha temple here is a pilgrim centre. A Monolithic statue of Bahubali 14metres high was erected here in 1973. Visitors are provided with free boarding and lodging by the temple authorities. There is a small museum, Manjusha Museum located opposite to the temple. There are two temple chariots covered in wooden figures and all types of religious objects including carved and painted panels, bronze sculptures and bells.
- Kollur, 147 km from Mangalore: The temple of goddess Mookambika is located here on top of Kodachadri hill, at the foot of the Western Ghats. The goddess takes the form of a 'Jyotirlinga' incorporating aspects of Shiva and Shakti. It is a pilgrimage centre attracting lot of devotees.
- Moodabidre: Situated 35 km from Mangalore, Moodabidire has Jain temples known as Basti's. There are 18 Bastis, the oldest and the largest is the Chandranatha Basti (1429) with its 1000 pillared hall. 'The Jain Matha' near the entrance has an important collection of manuscripts.

Other shrines worthy of mention are Shantinatha, Settara, Derama Setti Basti, Guru Basti, Kote and Vikrama Setti Basti.

- Bhatkal: located 135 km from Karwar was the main port of Vijayanagar empire in the 16th century. The ancient town has temples of Vijayanagar style and many Jain monuments. The 17th-century Hindu temple here in Vijayanagar style has animal carvings. 16 km away is the shore temple of Shri Murdeshwar. The temple attracts a lot of devotees and tourists.

Giant Shiva statue at Murdeshwara

- Honnavar: situated 90 km from Karwar, has a Portuguese fort. There is also a fort in Basavaraja Durga Island, amidst the sea which can be reached by a sail upstream on river Sharavathi.

- Ankola: Located 37 km south of Karwar, is a small town with 15th-century ruined walls of King Sarpamalika's fort and the ancient Shri Venketaraman Temple. Near the temple there are two giant wooden chariots carved with scenes from the *Ramayana*.
- Murudeshwar: The Murudeshwar Temple in Uttara Kannada District of Karnataka now possesses at 249-feet Raja Gopura. The Murudeswar temple complex is renowned for the tallest idol of Lord Shiva in the world, which is 123 feet. The latest addition to the temple, thanks to Mr. RN Shetty an entrepreneur and philanthropist, is the Rajagopuram, which was opened on 12 April 2008. And is it the tallest Hindu Temple Gopuram in the World. If Gopuram can be considered as a unique ornate structure associated with Hindu Temples, then the Gopura of Murudeshwar Temple in Karnataka should be the tallest in the world.

The Rajagopuram of Murudeswar Temple has 21 floors, including the ground floor. The base measures 105 feet in length and 51 feet breadth. The gopura also possess a lift and visitors can go to the top and have an aerial view of the Arabian Sea and the statue of Lord Shiva. Another highlight is the life-size statues of two elephants at the base of the gopura.

World's tallest Siva idol: The highlights of Murudeshwar lie beyond its beach and rural flair. On a little green hill, a 37 m (or 123 feet) Lord Shiva idol sits enthroned, surrounded by smaller statues illustrating moments of the Hindu mythology

Beaches

Karwar has a number of beaches like Blue Lagoon Beach, Ladies Beach around it and Rabindranath Tagore described his experiences at Karwar beach in his poetry. Om beach, Murdeshwara are other beaches of Uttara Kannada Dist. The Nethrani Island near Murdeshwara. Basavaraja Durga near Honavar is an island fort raised by the Keladi Rulers during 16th and 17th centuries. It is surrounded by a strong fortification raised by gigantic laterite blocks and the hill has a flat top.

Devagad and Kurmagad are two islands near Karwar. {Nirvana beach} at Kagal village of Kumta is a 5 km long beach in one stretch with white sand and transparent water in the month of December till March. The entire beach coastline is covered by Casuarina and coconut trees, unparallel to any beach of India, and has the big potential to develop beach tourism like the Baga-Calangute-Candolim beach of Goa. Government of Karnataka and tourism department has failed in tapping this potential, whereas Goa has left Karnataka much behind in beach tourism. There is an urgent need to do something in this direction to allow beach tourism on the same model of Goa in the months of September to may.

Planetarium

- Swami Vivekananda Planetarium: Situated at Pilikula in Mangalore, it is the 1st 3D Planetarium in India.

South Karnataka

South Karnataka is a unique combination of spectacular vesara style Hoysala architecture, colossal Jain monuments, colonial buildings and palaces of the Kingdom of Mysore, impregnable fort at Chitradurga and densely forested wildlife sanctuaries that offer some of the best eco-tourism available in the country. Belur, Halebidu in Hassan District, Somnathpura in Mysore District, Belavadi, Kalasa and Amrithapura in Chikmagalur District, Balligavi in Shimoga District offer some of the best of Hoysala architecture dating from the 11th to 13th centuries, while Shravanabelagola in Hassan district and Kambadahalli in Mandya District have well known 10th-century Jain monuments. Scenic forests and the high density of wild animals of this region are a popular attraction for those interested in the wilder side of life. Bandipur National Park, Nagarahole, Biligirirangan Hills, Bhadra Wildlife Sanctuary and Bannerghatta national parks are a few popular places for jungle safaris.

The river Kaveri flows east from Kodagu District and along its way one finds important tourist destinations like Shivanasamudra and nearby Sivasamudram Falls,

Srirangapattana and Melkote etc. Mysuru, the cultural capital of the state is home to palaces, colonial buildings and cultural activities including Carnatic music, theatre. Bengaluru the capital is a cosmopolitan city with parks, pubs, restaurants, shopping and fast-paced technology-rich lifestyle.

- Bengaluru: the capital of Karnataka has many tourist attractions.
- Mandya: is a city, Sugar factories contribute majorly to the economy of the city. The Mandir of Shri Shirdi Sai Baba popular amongst local Sai Devotees as Mandyada Shri Shiradi Sai Baba Mandir is situated at B.Gowdagere, Gejjalagere village amidsts picturesque natural surrounding in Mandya District of Karnataka. The Mandir is situated at a distance of about 9.3 kilometers from Maddur town and about 12 kilometers from Mandya Town on Bangalore-Mysore State Highway. All the buses playing on Bangalore-Mysore route stops at B.Gowdagere Sai Baba Mandir Entrance situated on the highway. The temple is situated at a distance of just 1 kilometre from the main road. The Mandir is lovingly addressed by everyone as "Namma Tatathana Mane" (Our Grand Father's Home).
- Belur: Home to the Hoysala temple complex. The Chennakeshava temple here was completed in 1116 by Hoysala Vishnuvardhana. The image is 3.7 m tall and the temple standing on a platform has exquisite plastic art work on its outer walls and bracket figures of dancing girls in various poses in perfect proportion. There are shrines of Kappe Chenniga Andal, Saumya Nayaki etc. The temple here is a classic example of Hoysala art, and Belur was one of the Hoysala Capitals.
- Halebidu: It is 27 km from Hassan, was capital of Hoysala and it was formerly called as Dwarasamudra. It has one of the finest Hoysala temples said to have been started by Ketamalla, a commander of Vishnuvardhana in 1121. The twin Shiva Temples, Hoysaleswara Temple and Kedareshwara Temple with a common platform and two

garbhagrihas, one houses for Vishnuvardhana Hoysaleshwara Linga and the other for Shanthaleshwara Linga. In front of Hoysaleshwara is the Nandimantapa and behind that is shrine of Surya with a two-meter-tall image. Outer walls have rows of intricate figures narrating episodes from epics like Ramyana, Mahabartha, and Bhagavata. There are also three Jain basadis equally rich in architecture. The temples are proposed to be listed under UNESCO World Heritage Sites.

Parshvanatha Basadi, Halebidu

- Arasikere: It is 41 km from Hassan and 176 km from Bangalore. It has coconut gardens. There is a Kattameshwara temple here which is also called Chandramoulishwara and referred to as Kalmeshwara in the records. It is a fine Hoysala monument with a rare polygonal frontal Mantapa with special design. There is a fine Haluvokkalu Temple and also a Sahasrakuta Jinalaya. Malekal Tirupathi near Arasikere has a venkataramana temple visited by many devotees.
- Aralaguppe: There is a Kalleshwara temple in the Ganga-Nalamba style of the 9th century. Its ceiling has a dancing

Shiva sculpture with musical accompanists and eight Dikpalas surrounding him with all their paraphernalia. There is a Chennakeshava temple of the Hoysala style. An image of Vishnu lies in the garbhagriha. There are four Ganga temples.

- Madhugiri: It is 43 km from Tumkur and has a large hill fort. The ancient name of the place is Maddagiri. It has the temples of Venkataramana and Malleshwara built by Vijayanagara feudatories. There is also a Mallinatha basadi. The fort has gateways called Antaralada Bagilu, Diddibagilu, Mysore Gate etc. 19 km from here is another hill fort called Midigeshi.
- Madikeri or Mercara: Known as Scotland of India, Mercara known for its climate. It has many places of attraction such as Tala Cauvery, Nagarahole National Park, Abbe Water Falls, St. Mark's Church, Bagamandala, Cauvery Nisargadhama, Belegiri Hills, Thadiyanda Murali Kund, Igguthappa Temple, Irupu Falls And Coffee & Tea Estates.

Gumbaz, Srirangapatna

- Srirangapattana: It is 14 km from Mysore & it is an island in between two branches of the Cauvery. It was also the capital of the Mysore rulers. There is a Ranganath temple here. The fort here was built in 1454. The Mysore rules made it their capital in 1610 in the days of Raja Wodeyar, who took it from the Vijayanagara Governor. The Ranganatha temple is called Adi Ranga. Ganjam has Dariya Daulat palace of Tipu and Gumbaz, the mausoleum of Haider and Tipu. Both are impressive structures of Indo-Saracenic style. The palace has paintings, fine woodwork and it houses a museum.

Temple complex on Chandragiri hill, Shravanabelagola

- Melukote: It is a religious centre which attracts lakhs of people during its annual feast Vairamudi. The temple was reconstructed in the Hoysala style by Visnuvardhana with the guidance of Ramanujacharya, a Visistadvaitist, in the 11th century. There are Cheluvanarayanaswamy temple, Kalyani, Hill shrine of Lord Narasimha, Thottilamadu, Dhanuskoti, Academy of Sanskrit Research and many more to visit. The nearest tourist places are Thondanur, Srirangapatna, Karigatta, Nagamangala etc.,

- Mahadeshwara Betta: It is 220 km from Bangalore and 142 km from Mysore. It is very close to eastern Ghats. It is said that a saint called Mahadeshwara, who could ride a tiger, lived and had his gadduge here during the 14th and 15th centuries. The hill is full of thick forests and thousands of pilgrims visit the place.
- Talakadu: A Holy place on the banks of the Cauvery. It is full of sands, carried by the wind from the dried bed of the river. It was the second capital of the Gangas. They built the Pataleshwara and the Maruleshwara templeshere. Hoysala Vishnuvardhana built Kirti Narayana temple.
- Bhadravathi: It is an industrial town in Shimoga district 256 km away from Bangalore, which was earlier known as "Benkipura". There is a 13th-century Lakshminarayan Temple in Hoysala style. An iron and steel works, a cement factory and a paper factory are located on the banks of Bhadra river.
- Ikkeri: It was a capital town of the Keladi Nayakas from 1512, and a place is 2 km from Sagara City. The Aghoreshwara temple is a 16th-century monument of great attraction. There is also a Paravathi temple nearby. Keladi is another place nearby, the original capital. It has the Rameshwara and Veerabhadra temples. There is also a museum.
- Sravanabelgola: It has a statue of Lord Bahubali. The place is an important Jain pilgrimage center and has a long history. The 17 meter high statue of Bahubali is said to be the tallest monolithic structure in the world. It overlooks the small town of Shravanbelgola from the top of the rocky hill known as Indragiri. One can reach this hill after ascending 614 rock-cut steps.
- Somnathpura: It is the home to one of the best examples of Hoysala temple architecture, the Kesava Temple.
- Jog Falls: the highest waterfalls in India, is located about 30 km from Sagara City, Karnataka. The Sharavati river

drops 253 metres in 4 separate falls known as Rani-the Rocket and Raja-the Roarer. The highest is the Raja with the fall of 253 metres and a pool below 40metres deep. The best time to visit is Late November to early January. The 50 km long Hirebhasgar Reservoir and the Linganamkki dam regulates the flow of the Sharavati river to generate the hydro electricity.

- Mekedatu: It is a picnic spot by the river Cauvery. It tumbles down through a deep ravine, on top of which is a chasm around 5 meters wide. Mekedatu is on Kanakapura Road.
- Hesaraghatta: Hesaraghatta has an artificial lake, a dairy and a horticulture farm. Boating and windsurfing are the other attractions. Also here is the Nrityagrama where young dancers are trained in all disciplines of traditional dance.
- Shivagange: A hill with four faces, rising to a height of 4599 ft looks like a Nandi from the East, Ganesh from the West, A Linga from the South and Cobra with it hood spread from the North side. It is accessible by road.
- Shivanasamudram: The waterfalls, the Ganganchukki and the Bharachukki, cascade down 90 meters. These falls are the source of Asia's first Hydro Electric Power Statin called "Shimsa". The falls are in full splendour during July–August. The falls are 22 km from the Bangalore.
- Hogenakkal Falls: These are also known as the 'smoking rocks' because of the mist. At the bottom of the 90 ft water falls, one can ride in a coracle.
- Devarayanadurga: This is a hill station of Tumkur road perched at a height of 3940 feet. A few kilometres from foot of the hills is a natural spring called Namada Chilume.

Palaces

- Bangalore Palace
- Mysore Palace,Also known as Ambavilas Palace

- Nalknad Palace
- Rajendra Vilas
- Jaganmohan Palace
- Jayalakshmi Vilas Mansion
- Lalitha Mahal
- Rajendra Vilas
- Cheluvamba Mansion, Mysore
- Shivappa Nayaka Palace
- Daria Daulat Bagh

Forts

In Karnataka there are thousands of Forts, in Kannada called as *Kote* or *Gad* or *Durga*.

Mirjan Fort in Uttara Kannada District in North Karnataka

The Forts in Karnataka are belongs to various dynasties, some of them are more than thousand years old.

Caves

Some well known caves in Karnataka are Yana caves and Kavala caves and Syntheri rocks in Uttara Kannada district, Sugriva's cave in Hampi holds similarity to the descriptions of 'Kishkinda' in the epic Ramayana, hundreds of caves in Basava Kalyana in Bidar District.

Ravana Phadi cave, Aihole in Karnataka

- Aihole
- Badami cave temples
- Gavi Gangadhareshwara Temple
- Nellitheertha Cave Temple
- Hulimavu Shiva cave temple
- Pandava caves Mangalore
- Savandurga
- Kavala Caves
- Anthargange

Waterfalls

Gaganachukki Falls at Shivanasamudram

Karnataka has a number of waterfalls. Jog Falls of Sagara Taluk is one of the highest waterfalls in Asia. Some well known waterfalls are Varapoha Falls, Magod Falls, Lalgulli Falls, Sathodi Falls, Unchalli Falls, Lushington Falls, Shivaganga Falls, Ulavi Falls, Irupu Falls, Sivasamudram Falls near Shivanasamudra, Balmuri Falls, Gokak Falls, Abbe Falls, Achakanya Falls, Chunchanakatte Falls, Hebbe Falls, Kallathigiri Falls, Sogal Falls, Godachinamalki Falls etc.

- Gokak Falls, Ghataprabha River, near Gokak, Belgaum district: It drops from 52 metres over a sand-stone cliff in a gorge. It is known locally as "mini Niagara" Hydro Electric Power has been harnessed at the falls since 1887 to run a cotton mill. Temples near the falls date from Badami Chalukyas to later Chalukya times and Vijayanagara periods. A suspension bridge crosses the river
- Godachinamalki Falls, Markhandeya River, near Godachinamalki, Belgaum district.
- Lushington Falls, Aghanashini River, Siddhapur Taluk: 116 meters in height and named after a district collector who discovered them in 1845
- Magod Falls, Gangavathi River, 125 km from Karwar: 183 metres (600 feet) in height, consists of a series of cascades over cliffs
- Varapoha Falls, Mahadayi River, in the Jamboti forest

8

Population and Religion

POPULATION OF KARNATAKA

Karnataka is a state located in south India. It was encircled on 1 November 1956, with the area of the States Reorganization Act. At first known as the State of Mysore, it was renamed Karnataka in 1973. The capital of Karnataka is Bangalore. The state is especially connected in roadways, railways and aviation routes. It also has some private air terminals as well.

It is the seventh biggest Indian state by an area. With 61,130,704 inhabitants at the 2011 assessment, Karnataka is the eighth biggest state in terms of population, containing 30 areas. Kannada, one of the set up dialects of India is the most comprehensively spoken language out here. The state is an incredible place to go on an excursion with your loved ones as it offers a considerable measure of things for each age group.

Population Of Karnataka In 2018

As per the 2011 registration of India, the aggregate population of the state was 61,095,297 of which (50.7%) were male and about (49.3%) were female.

Talking about population, in order to check out the population of Karnataka in 2018, we need to have a look at the population of the past 5 years. They are as per the following:

1. 2013 – 62.8 Million
2. 2014 – 64.06 Million

3. 2015 – 65.8 Million
4. 2016 – 66 Million
5. 2017 – 66.8 Million

Predicting the 2018 population of Karnataka is not easy but we can get the idea after analysing the population from the year 2013 – 17. As we have seen that every year the population increases by approximate 0.8 Million people. Hence, the population of Karnataka in 2018 is forecast to be 66.8 Million + 0.8 Million = 67.6 Million. So, the population of Karnataka in the year 2018 as per estimated data is 67.6 Million.

Karnataka Population 2018 –67.6 Million. (estimated).

Demography Of Karnataka:

The literacy rate of Karnataka was 75.36% as per the last data records. 84.00% of its people were Hindu, 13% Muslim, 1.9% Christian, 0.16% Buddhist and 0.05% were Sikh. Also, 0.27% of the population did not tell their religion.

Kannada is the official lingo of the state and it is spoken by 66.26% of the overall public. Different minorities in the state are Urdu, Telegu, Tamil, Hindi and Malayalam. In 2007 the state had a birth rate of 2.2% and a death rate of about 0.2%. The total fertility rate of Karnataka was 2.2.

Population Density And Growth Of Karnataka:

The population density of the state is 319 persons per square kilometre. The number of people living per square kilometer in the city has extended to 4,378 in the year 2011 from 2,985 in 2001, as shown by the assessment data released. The number of people in the state has grown basically in 2011 when contrasted with that of 2001. The growth in terms of population is an outcome of adding six new fringe domains to Bangalore.

Facts About Karnataka:

1. In Karnataka, 83% are Hindus and 11% of the populations are Muslims and remaining others consolidates Christian, Buddhist and Jain etc.
2. The state is especially connected in roadways, railways

and aviation routes. It also has some private air terminals as well. These are in Bangalore, Belgaum, Mangalore and so on.

3. The state is surrounded by the Arabian Sea, Maharashtra, Goa, Tamil Nadu and Kerala.
4. It is the place where the two central conduit frameworks of India stream out to the Bay of Bengal.
5. In November 1956, Karnataka was made by the States Reorganization Act and named it as State of Mysore. During 1973 it was renamed to Karnataka.

DEMOGRAPHICS

According to the 2011 census of India, the total population of Karnataka was 61,095,297 of which 30,966,657 (50.7%) were male and 30,128,640 (49.3%) were female, or 1000 males for every 973 females. This represents a 15.60% increase over the population in 2001. The population density was 319 per km^2 and 38.67% of the people lived in urban areas. The literacy rate was 75.36% with 82.47% of males and 68.08% of females being literate. 84.00% of the population were Hindu, 12.92% were Muslim, 1.87% were Christian, 0.72% were Jains, 0.16% were Buddhist, 0.05% were Sikh and 0.02% were belonging to other religions and 0.27% of the population did not state their religion.

Kannada is the official language of Karnataka and spoken as a native language by about 66.54% of the people as of 2011. Other linguistic minorities in the state were Urdu (10.83%), Telugu (5.84%), Tamil (3.45%), Marathi (3.38%), Hindi (3.3%), Tulu (2.61%), Konkani (1.29%), Malayalam (1.27%) and Kodava Takk (0.18%). In 2007 the state had a birth rate of 2.2%, a death rate of 0.7%, an infant mortality rate of 5.5% and a maternal mortality rate of 0.2%. The total fertility rate was 2.2.

In the field of speciality health care, Karnataka's private sector competes with the best in the world. Karnataka has also established a modicum of public health services having a better record of health care and child care than most other states of India. In spite of these advances, some parts of the state still leave much to be desired when it comes to primary health care.

Demographics of Karnataka

Karnataka, with a total population of 61,100,000, is one of the major states in South India. Kannada is the official language of Karnataka. Other linguistic minorities in the state are Tulu, Kodava, Konkani, Urdu, Telugu, Marathi, Tamil, Hindi and Malayalam. Karnataka is also in the forefront of population control measures with the world's first two birth controlclinics being set up in 1930 in the Mandya district.

Population

According to the 2011 census of India, the total population of Karnataka is 6.25 crores. Of this, 50.9% are male and 49.1% are female. There is a decadal increase in population of 17.3% from 1991 to 2001. As per 2011 census, the Population density is 319 per km^2, the sex ratio is 973 females to 1000 males and 38.67% of the people in Karnataka live in urban areas. The literacy rate is 75.4% (as per the 2011 census). As per the 2001 census, the eight largest cities of Karnataka in order of their population are Bengaluru, Hubballi-Dharwad, Mysuru, Belagavi, Kalburgi, Mangaluru, Davanagere and Ballari. The state has one of the largest populations of Anglo-Indians in India. Given below is a composite table of languages and religions of Karnataka at the census 2001 languages in karnataka

Religion in Karnataka

Hindu	84.2%
Muslim	12.9%
Christian	1.9%
Others	1.0%

Bengaluru Urban and Belagavi are the most populous Districts, each of them having a population of more than three million. Gadaga, Chamarajanagara and Kodagu districts have a population of less than a million.

According to 2011 Census of India, 84% of the population are Hindu, 12.9% are Muslim, 1.9% are Christian, 0.7% are Jains, 0.2% are Buddhist, <0.1% are Sikhs, and remaining belong to other religions. Karnataka is also the location of some of tribes like, Nayaka, Soliga, and Yerava. The joint family system is prevalent in the rural areas of Karnataka and there are extreme cases like the Narasinganavars who reside in the Dharwad district and are recognised as one of the largest undivided families in the world.

Languages

Government Census (2001) Kannada 68.5 %, Urdu 10.5 %, Telugu 5.0 %, Marathi 3.3 %, Tamil 3.2 %, Tulu 2.8 %, Hindi 2.6%, Konkani 1.5 %, Malayalam 1.3 %, other 0.8 %.

Health care

The princely state of Mysore was the first state in India to take up a vaccination drive against smallpox. World's first two birth control clinics were set up in Karnataka in the district of Mandya. Even though health care in Karnataka's private sector is among world's best, state as a whole has not been fully successful in providing effective primary health care. Apart from capital Bangalore and coastal districts of Udupi and Dakshina Kannada other parts of the state especially northern districts have not received sufficient attention by government and private sectors. However Karnataka has established a modicum of public health services having a better record of health care and child care compared to other states of India. The state has a birth rate of 2.2%, death rate of 0.7%, an infant mortality rate of 5.5%, a maternal mortality rate of 0.2% and 2.2 being total fertility rate. In 2004 state's Health and Family Welfare Services had 8,143 sub-centres (one for 5,000 people), 581 Primary Health Units (PHUs), 1,679 Primary Health Centres (PHCs), 19 mobile units, 7,304 maternity annexes, 17 urban PHCs and 110 Community Health Centres. There were 87 Urban Family Welfare Centres, 124 Urban Health Centres and 24 district level and 149 taluk level hospitals. Six government hospitals in Karnataka have won ISO-9002 certification. During 2004-05 Karnataka slipped from the sixth place to the seventh in the Human Development Index. During fiscal year 2004-05, only 0.7% of total GSDP was allocated to health sector.

Karnataka is one of the states of India most seriously affected by the HIV/AIDS epidemic and stands fifth on the number of reported AIDS cases in the country. The first case of AIDS was detected in the state in 1988. Of the 49 high prevalence HIV/AIDS districts in India, 10 are in Karnataka. This has caused Karnataka to become the first state in India to bring in legislation making pre-marital HIV tests compulsory. In 2010, the Government of Karnataka approved new state-of-the-art HIV/AIDS prevention education developed at Stanford University by U.S. nonprofit TeachAIDS, and committed to distributing them in 5,500 government schools.

Karnataka is also home to Handigodu Syndrome, a rare and painful osteoarthritic disorder endemic to the Malnad region of the state.

KARNATAKA ETHNIC GROUPS

Karnataka is a state in the southern part of India. It was created on 1 November 1956, with the passing of the States Reorganisation Act. Karnataka is bordered by the Arabian Sea to the west, Goa to the north-west, Maharashtra to the north, Telangana and Andhra Pradesh to the east, Tamil Nadu to the south-east, and Kerala to the south-west. The state covers an area of 74,122 sq mi (191,976 km^2), or 5.83% of the total geographical area of India. It comprises 30 districts. Kannada is the official language of Karnataka and is spoken as a native language by about 74% of the people. Various ethnic groups with origins in other parts of India have unique customs and use languages at home other than Kannada, adding to the cultural diversity of the state. Other ethnic minorities in the state in 1991 were Urdu people(9.72%), Telugu people (6.34%), Tamil people (5.46%) Marathi people (3.95%), Tuluvas (3.38%), Hindi (1.87%), Konkani people (1.78%), Malayalis (1.69%), Kodavas (0.25%), and Gujarati people (0.10%).

Kannadiga

Kannadigas form the dominant ethnic group in Karnataka, making up to 72% of the total population of the state. They are the native speakers of the Kannada language. Kannada is one of the official languages of India and the official and administrative language of the state of Karnataka. Based on the recommendations of the Committee of Linguistic Experts, appointed by the Ministry of Culture, the Government of India officially recognised Kannada as a classical language.

Tuluva people

Tuluvas are the native speakers of Tulu language. They form the dominant ethnic community in the districts of Dakshina Kannada and Udupiof Karnataka and Kasargod Taluk of Kerala, which is often termed as a single region called as Tulu Nadu. Yakshagana, Nagaradhane, Bootha Kola and Aati kalenja are the distinctive features of Tuluva culture. Tuluvas follow a matrilineal system of inheritance known as Aliyasantana which has given them a unique cultural status. As per the 1991 census, Tuluvas formed 2.38% of the total population of the state.

Konkani people

The speakers of Konkani language are widely settled in the districts of Uttara Kannada, Udupi and Dakshina Kannada (Udupi and Dakshina Kannada were the erstwhile South Canara district). In Karwar Taluk (Uttara Kannada district) alone, Konkani language is spoken by about 78% of the population. Significant population of Konkani people has also settled in Belgaum, Sirsi and Bangalore. As per the 1991 census, speakers of Konkani form 1.78% of the total population of the state. In Karnataka, which has the largest number of Konkanis, leading organizations and activists have similarly demanded that Kannada script be made the medium of instruction for Konkani in local schools instead of Devanagari. Most Konkani-speaking people of the state are bilingual in Kannada and Tulu.

Kodava people

Kodava people are the native speakers of Kodava language and are of a martial race mainly settled in the district of Kodagu. As per the 1991 census, the speakers of Kodava Takk make up up to 0.25% of the total population of the state.

According to Karnataka Kodava Sahitya Academy, apart from Kodavas, 18 other ethnic groups speak Kodava Takk in and outside the district including Heggade, Iri, Koyava, Banna, kudiya, Kembatti, and Meda. Though the language has no script, recently German linguist Gregg M. Cox developed a new writing system for the language known as the Coorgi-Cox alphabet, used by a number of individuals in Kodagu. Lately, some organizations including the Codava National Council (CNC)'and Kodava Rashtriya Samiti are demanding Kodava homeland status and autonomy for Kodagu district.

Religions

	Kannada	Other languages	Total
Hindu	70.9%	15%	83.9%
Muslim	1.2%	9%	12.2%
Christian	1%	0.9%	1.9%
Other religions	1%	1%	2%
Total	74.1%	25.9%	100%

Urdu

People speaking Urdu as their mother tongue form the second largest ethnic group in Karnataka (9.72% of the total population as per the 1991 census), the majority of whom are Muslims (constituting 85.6% of the Muslim population in Karnataka). The concentration of speakers of Urdu shows an uneven distribution over different districts in Karnataka. The difference in the numerical strength of Urdu speakers varies from a few hundred to thousands. Almost 57.5% of the total Urdu population in Karnataka are bilingual. Kannada is the most preferred language among the Urdu speakers of Karnataka. About 43.5% of the total Urdu population has bilingualism in Kannada.

Tamil people

Tamil people are the native speakers of the Tamil language, which is spoken predominantly in the adjoining state of Tamil

Nadu. The language has official status in the Indian state of Tamil Nadu and in the Indian union territory of Puducherry. Tamil is also an official language of Sri Lanka, Singapore, Malaysia, Mauritius and Fiji Islands. It is one of the twenty-two scheduled languages of India and the first Indian language to be declared as a classical language by the government of India in 2004. Tamil is also spoken by significant minorities in Malaysia, Myanmar, Mauritius, South Africa, Trinidad and Tobago and Réunion as well as emigrant communities around the world.

Bharatanatyam is a classical dance form of India which has its origin in south India, and it is immensely popular in Karnataka as well.

In Karnataka however, Tamils form 5.46% of the total population of the state. There has been a recorded presence of Tamil-speaking people in Southern Karnataka since the 10th century. During the eleventh century AD, the areas in and around Bangalore were a bone of contention between the Tamil-speaking Cholas and the Kannada-speaking Western Chalukyas. The Vaishnavite Brahmins of Southern Karnataka use the Tamil surname "Iyengar" and are believed to have migrated during the time of the 12th century Vaishnavite saint Ramanujacharya. Most Iyengars in Karnataka use sub-dialects of Iyengar Tamil.

After the fall of Tipu Sultan, a large British Army presence in the Cantonment area (Bangalore) attracted speakers of Tamil, who either were attached to the military or were military suppliers.In fact, the area was administered directly by the Madras Presidency, and was handed over to the Mysore State only in 1949. Today, the erstwhile Cantonment area of Bangalore comprising Ulsoor, Shivajinagar, Benson Town, Richard's Town, Frazer Town, Austin Town, Richmond Town, Cox Town, Murphy Town and others still boast a large Tamil populace. The boom in the textile industry in the early part of 20th Century also witnessed migration from the Madras Presidency. Some of the very well known mills of the time employed Tamil-speaking people in large numbers, who settled down in areas in and around Bangalore

Tamil-speaking people are largely found in the districts of Bangalore Urban, Bangalore Rural, Shivamogga, Ramanagara, Mysore, Kolar, Hassan, Mandya and Chamarajanagar in southern Karnataka, Tungabadhra Dam [Bellary district | Hospet] in North Karnataka. Recent migrants speak Tamil while older migrants are bilingual in Kannada and Tamil. In 1991, Tamils constituted the largest ethnolinguistic minority in Bangalore city making up 21.38% of the total population. Today, Tamil speakers form an estimated 18-25% of the population of Bangalore city. As of 1971, Tamil formed the second-largest mother tongue in Bangalore and Bhadravathi, third in Mysore and Shimoga, fourth in Davanagereand fifth in Mangalore. The districts, according to the 1971 census, where the largest proportion of Karnataka's Tamil population live are Bangalore (53.7 percent of the Tamil-speaking population of Karnataka), Kolar (14 percent) and Mysore (8.6 percent).

There are also Tamil families from Sri Lanka who were originally of South Indian Tamil descent, settled in Sulya and Puttur taluks of Dakshina Kannada district and are currently working in rubber plantations in the district.

RELIGION

Religion in Karnataka (2011)

Hinduism	84.00%
Islam	12.92%
Christianity	1.87%
Jainism	0.72%
Buddhism	0.16%
Sikhism	0.05%
Other	0.02%
Not religious	0.27%

Vishnu, Badami cave temple no.3

Adi Shankaracharya (788–820) chose Sringeri in Karnataka to establish the first of his four *mathas* (monastery). Madhvacharya (1238–1317) was the chief proponent of Tattvavada (Philosophy of Reality), popularly known as Dvaita or Dualistic school of Hindu philosophy — one of the three most influential Vedanta philosophies. Madhvacharya was one of the important philosophers during the Bhakti movement.

Gomateswara (982–983) at Shravanabelagola is an important centre of Jain pilgrimage.

He was a pioneer in many ways, going against standard conventions and norms. According to tradition, Madhvacharya is believed to be the third incarnation of Vayu(Mukhyaprana), after Hanuman and Bhima. The Haridasa devotional movement is considered as one of the turning points in the cultural history of India. Over a span of nearly six centuries, several saints and mystics helped shape the culture, philosophy and art of South India and Karnataka in particular by exerting considerable spiritual influence over the masses and kingdoms that ruled South India.

This movement was ushered in by the Haridasas (literally "servants of Lord Hari") and took shape in the 13th century – 14th century CE, period, prior to and during the early rule of the Vijayanagara empire. The main objective of this movement was to propagate the Dvaita philosophy of Madhvacharya

(Madhva Siddhanta) to the masses through a literary medium known as Dasa Sahitya literature of the servants of the Lord. Purandaradasa is widely recognised as the *"Pithamaha"* of Carnatic Music for his immense contribution. Ramanujacharya, the leading expounder of *Vishishtadvaita*, spent many years in Melkote. He came to Karnataka in 1098 AD and lived here until 1122 AD. He first lived in Tondanur and then moved to Melkote where the Cheluvanarayana Swamy Temple and a well-organised *matha* were built. He was patronised by the Hoysala king, Vishnuvardhana.

In the twelfth century, Lingayatism emerged in northern Karnataka as a protest against the rigidity of the prevailing social and caste system. Leading figures of this movement were Basava, Akka Mahadevi and Allama Prabhu, who established the Anubhava Mantapa which was the centre of all religious and philosophical thoughts and discussions pertaining to Ligayats. These three social reformers did so by the literary means of *"Vachana Sahitya"* which is very famous for its simple, straight forward and easily understandable Kannada language. Lingayatism preached women equality by letting women wear *Ishtalinga* i.e. Symbol of god around their neck. Basava shunned the sharp hierarchical divisions that existed and sought to remove all distinctions between the hierarchically superior master class and the subordinate, servile class. He also supported inter-caste marriages and Kaayaka Tatva of Basavanna. This was the basis of the Lingayat faith which today counts millions among its followers.

The Jain philosophy and literature have contributed immensely to the religious and cultural landscape of Karnataka. Islam, which had an early presence on the west coast of India as early as the tenth century, gained a foothold in Karnataka with the rise of the Bahamani and Bijapur sultanates that ruled parts of Karnataka. Christianity reached Karnataka in the sixteenth century with the arrival of the Portuguese and St. Francis Xavier in 1545.

Buddhism was popular in Karnataka during the first millennium in places such as Gulbarga and Banavasi. A chance discovery of edicts and several Mauryan relics at Sannati in

Gulbarga district in 1986 has proven that the Krishna River basin was once home to both Mahayana and Hinayana Buddhism. There are Tibetan refugee camps in Karnataka.

Festivals

Mysore Dasara is celebrated as the *Nada habba* (state festival) and this is marked by major festivities at Mysore. *Ugadi* (Kannada New Year), *Makara Sankranti* (the harvest festival), *Ganesh Chaturthi*, *Gowri Habba*, *Ram Navami*, *Nagapanchami*, *Basava Jayanthi*, *Deepavali*, and *Ramzan* are the other major festivals of Karnataka.

RELIGION IN KARNATAKA

Religion in Karnataka (2011)

Hinduism (84.00%)

Islam (12.92%)

Christianity (1.87%)

Jainism (0.72%)

Buddhism (0.16%)

Sikhism (0.05%)

Other (0.02%)

Not religious (0.27%)

Religion in Karnataka has played a very important role in shaping modern Indian religions and philosophy.

Hinduism

The three most important schools of Vedanta Hinduism, Advaita Vedanta, Vishishtadvaita and Dvaita, blossomed in Karnataka. The Dvaita Madhvacharya was born in Karnataka. The Advaita Adi Shankara chose Shringeri in Karnataka to establish the first of his four mathas. The Vishishtadvaita Ramanuja, considered a saint in Sri Sampradaya, who fled persecution by the Shaiva Chola dynasty of Tamil Nadu, spent from 1098-1122 in Karnataka. He first lived in Tondanur and then moved to Melukote where the Cheluvanarayana Swamy Temple and a well-organised matha were built. He was patronized by Hoysala Vishnuvardhana. Udupi, Shringeri,

Gokarna and Melukote are well known places of Sanskrit and Vedic learning.

In the 12th century, social reforms emerged in northern Karnataka as a protest against the rigidity of the prevailing social and caste system. Leading figures of the movement such as Basava, Akka Mahadevi and Allama Prabhu established the Anubhava Mantapa where Lingayatism was expounded. Nearly 17% population of Karnataka belongs to Lingayat sect. In 2018, the Government of Karnataka has given its nod to form Lingayatism as a separate religion, but it is still waiting for approval from central government. .

Jainism

Jainism had a stronghold in Karnataka in the early medieval period at Shravanabelagola as its most important centre. The first Tirthankara, Rishabha, is said to have spent his final days in Karnataka. Both Jain philosophy and literature have contributed immensely to the religious and cultural landscape of Karnataka. Jain influence on literature and philosophy is particularly evident. Shravanabelgola, Moodabidri, and Karkala are famous for Jain history and monuments.

Buddhism

Buddhism was once popular in Karnataka during the first millennium in places such as Gulbarga and Banavasi. A chance discovery of edicts and several Mauryan relics at Sannati in the Gulbarga district in 1986 has proven that the Krishna river basin was once home to both Mahayanaand Theravada Buddhism. In recent times, Buddhism thrives here and calls Dzogchen monastery and the Dhondeling Tibetan refugee camps as home.

Culture

Karnataka played a very important role in shaping present day Indian religion and philosophy. Udupi, Sringeri, Gokarna and Melukote are well known places of Sanskrit learning and Vedic learning. Shravanabelagola, Mudabidri, Karkala are famous for Jain history and monuments.

The great saint Madhvacharya (1238-1317 AD), proponent of dvaita philosophy and Raghavendra Swami were born here. Adi Sankara, proponent of advaita found enlightenment in Sringeri which became the first of four mathas he established in India. Fearing persecution from the Tamil CholasRamanujacharya fled Tamil Nadu and came to Karnataka during the rule of the Hoysala dynasty and preached his philosophy from Melukote. In the 12th century AD, Virashaivism spread from northern Karnataka across the Deccan. Many of its founders, such as Basavanna, Akka Mahadevi came from the region. It was here the Jain religion got a warm welcome and enjoyed a glorious growth during the medieval period. It is also here where the current day Dzogchen Monastery and the Dhondeling Tibetan Refugee camps are set up and the Tibetans are very well absorbed in the Kannadiga culture.

Temples

The Empires and Kingdoms that came to rule from Karnataka were prolific builders. The Badami Chalukyas spawned the *Vesara* style of architecture and experimented with several myriad styles with frequent intermixing of *Nagara* and Dravida concepts. This period is the beginning of Hindu rock cut architecture, both in stand alone and cave temple idioms, numerous examples of which exist in Pattadakal, Aihole and Badami - (Badami Cave Temples). Their successors, the Rashtrakuta created master piece temples further favoring Dravidian concepts. Most of their temples in Karnataka are scattered over northern Karnataka districts. The Ganga Dynasty of Talakad built many Jaina monuments including the monolithic statue of Gomateshwara at Shravanabelagola. The Western Chalukyas used the *In-between* style, implying a bridge between Chalukya - Rashtrakuta and Hoysala styles, with the best temples of their style located in the central districts of Gadag district(Lakkundi, Dambal, Sudi, Lakshmeshwar, Gadag), Koppal district(Mahadeva Temple (Itagi), Kuknur), Haveri district (Galaganatha, Chaudayyadanapura, Haveri, Harlahalli, Hangal) and Dharwad District (Annigeri, Kundgol, Tamboor, Chandramouleshwara Temple Unakal Hubli). It was during the reign of the Hoysalas that the temple architecture reached its epoch and gained recognition as an independent style called (Henry Ferguson, Percy Brown) owing to its many unique features. Later the Vijayanagar Empire would incorporate all these various styles and create a unique blend called Vijayanagar style, the best examples of which are in the vast open air theater of monuments at Hampi.

Islam and Christianity

Islam, which had an early presence in the west coast of India as early as the 10th century gained a foothold in Karnataka with the arrival of the Bahmani Sultanate and Adil Shahi dynasty, which ruled parts of Karnataka.

Christianity reached Karnataka in the 16th century with the arrival of the Portuguese and St. Francis Xavier in 1545.

Today, Islam and Christianity have a sizable following in Karnataka and have contributed to the cultural cosmopolitanism of the state.

Islam

Islam arrived in Karnataka and Kerala in the 7th century with Arab merchants trading in spices. Muslims introduced coffee, incense sticks and the paper industry to the local economy. Following the 12th century, various invading Islamic armies established sultanates in this area such as the Bahamani sultanate of Bidar (1347–1510) and the Adilshahi dynasty of the Bijapur Sultanate (1490–1686).

This land came under Mughal rule in the 17th century under Aurangzeb's rule. With the disintegration of Mughal rule, Hyder Ali and his son Tippu Sultanestablished their rule over the Mysore area. They violently resisted British rule in the area, but without adequate cooperation from other kingdoms, were defeated.

Though killed by the British in 1799, Tippu Sultan was one of the only Indian leaders to defeat the British in battle, which made him as a iconic leader among the people in the modern era.In addition, the Nizams of Hyderabad ruled over large parts of Northeastern Karnataka. This land only became part of Karnataka after the passing of the 1956 States Reorganisation

Act.

Muslims form approximately 12.91% of the population of Karnataka. While Muslims can be found in all districts of Karanataka, Muslims have a stronger presence in:

1. Northern Karnataka (especially in the area formerly ruled by the Princely State of Hyderabad) such as Gulbarga, Bidar, Bijapur, Raichur and Dharwad.
2. The districts bordering Kerala such as Dakshina Kannada and Kodagu where Muslim Mappila presence is strong.
3. The cities of Bangalore, Mysore and Mangalore.

On the other hand, the proportion of Muslims is lower in central Karnataka. The main spoken language of Muslims in Karnataka is Urdu, spoken in the Dakhni accent. Most Muslims in Karnataka also speak Kannada, Telugu and Sindhi. There are a large number of Muslim run educational institutions in Karnataka. Muslims also have modestly higher levels of progress in terms of education and wealth in Karnataka (as in the rest of South India) than in states of North India, as they are comparatively given more opportunities than their North Indian counterparts.

Christianity

Christianity arrived in Karnataka between 1500-1600 CE with the Portuguese. the majority of Christians found in west coast of Karnataka that is from Karwar to Mangalore.

Mangalore has the largest population of Roman Catholics as compared to other parts of Karnataka. They are mostly descended from Goan Catholics who immigrated from Goa in the 17th and 18th centuries. There are also some Protestants found in Karnataka. Many of them are of local origin. Protestants are the result of British missionaries' work during the British empire in India. However the British conversion was voluntary and not compulsory as Portuguese was in most cases. Due to this the Protestants are less in number as compared to the Catholics. Bangalore has a large number of Catholics as well as Protestant people.

HINDUISM IN KARNATAKA

Hinduism is the third largest religion of the world and the most observed religious traditions of India. It is the largest religion in Karnataka, the southwest Indian state. Several great empires and dynasties have ruled over Karnataka and many of them have contributed richly to the growth of Hinduism, its temple culture and social development. These developments have reinforced the "Householder tradition", which is of disciplined domesticity, though the saints who propagated Hinduism in the state and in the country were themselves ascetics. The Bhakti movement, of Hindu origin, is devoted to the worship of Shiva and Vishnu; it had a telling impact on the sociocultural ethos of Karnataka from the 12th century onwards.

Movements

Karnataka was the birthplace of several notable Hindu movements. The three most prominent movements of Vedanta Hinduism — Advaita Vedanta, Vishishtadvaita and Dvaita— began in Karnataka. The Dvaita Madhvacharya, who was from Karnataka, was the chief proponent of Tattvavâda, the "philosophy of reality". The Advaita Adi Shankara chose Sringeri in Karnataka to establish the first of his four mathas. The Vishishtadvaita philosopher Ramanuja, considered a saint in Sri Sampradaya, fled from persecution by the Shaiva Chola dynasty of Tamil Nadu, and stayed in Karnataka from 1098–1122. He first lived in Tondanur and then shifted to Melukote where the Cheluvanarayana Swamy Temple and a well-organised *math* (religious centre) were established. He was patronized by Hoysala Vishnuvardhana. Udupi, Shringeri, Gokarna and Melukote are also well known places of Sanskrit and Vedic learning.

Lingayatism

Hinduism is the largest religion in Karnataka, followed by Buddhism, Christianity, Jainism, Islam and Sikhism. According to the 2011 census, 84.00% of the state's population practices Hinduism. In the past, Jainism dominated Hinduism. In the 12th century, Lingayatism emerged in northern Karnataka as a protest against the rigidity of the prevailing social and caste system. Leading figures of the movement, such as Basava, Akka Mahadevi and Allama Prabhu, established the Anubhava Mantapa where Lingayatism was expounded. This was to form the basis of the Lingayat faith and its followers, the Lingayats, account for 17% of the total population of 65 million in Karnataka. When the Lingayat sect came to be established in Karnataka, the then prospering Jain community's practice of Jainism became ineffectual as a religious practice in the state. Ligayats hold a considerable sway in Karnataka to this day.

Bhakti

Under the Bhakti movement, Vishnu and Shiva were the main focus of devotion by both Lingayat and Brahminical communities. The devotional movement in Hinduism is divine grace and is known as the Bhakti movement. Basava (1106–1167), also called Basavanna, protested against caste system and was for equality among all classes. His movement was called the Bhakti Movement and it had a profound paradigm shift in the socio-cultural ethos of the state of Karnataka. The basic tenet of this philosophy, propounded from the 12th century by the Virashaiva school or Virashaivism, was opposition to the caste system, rejection of the supremacy of the Brahmins, abhorrence to ritual sacrifice, and insistence on Bhakti and the worship of the one God, Shiva. His followers were called Virashaivas, meaning "stalwart Shiva-worshipers". Before the start of this movement, the Bhakti tradition had taken deep roots in Tamil Nadu which permeated to Karnataka. The Ligayat or Virashaiva sect were the forerunners in this movement. They abhorred caste system and were emphatic to practice the direct interaction with god and symbolically express it through wearing small linga around their neck signifying their faith. The Shaiva Siddhanta, which was practiced in Tamil Nadu and which included tantric practices also formed the base line for the Lingayat religion. But their religious ethos was not to the liking of other Hindu groups.

Allama Prabhu a poet saint in the 12th century of the Lingayat sect, was a contemporary of Basava. Allama was instrumental in prompting bhakti cult through his poems in Kannada language among Shiva worshipers. This was an enlightened way of worship in which caste distinctions were discarded. It was believed that Allama was incarnate of Lord Shiva and hence he was given the epithet 'Prabhu' which was suffixed to his name. His poems were totally devotional and expressed in his status of achieving detachment from rituals.

Lakula, Kalamukha, and Kapalikas

In Karnataka before the Lingayats' started their bhakthi movement, there was the Kalamukha sect who were worshipers of Shiva. They practiced the movement from the 11th century. They were also opposed to asceticism like the Lingayats. The Kalamukha were a sub-sect of the Lakula Sect, who had lot of influence over the people. They collected funds for their temples and mathas (monastic centers). The Kalamukha ascetic sect was popular during the 9th to 13th centuries, but is now extinct. They painted their faces with a black streak and were contemporary to another sect known as Kapalikas. Their religious dogmas are not clear except for some inscriptions which attest to their strong influence in Karnataka.

Haridasas

Another bhakthi movement established in the 13th century was of Haridasas, a devotional group of saints who formed the group under the same name, and who were Vaishnavites of the Dwiata philosophy. The founder of this movement was Naraharitirtha, a devout Madhvafollower. Their worship is devoted to various forms of Lord Vishnu or Hari. This Bhakthi cult's propagation was not only worship of Vishnu but also to discard animal sacrifice, stop beliefs in superstitions, discourage caste system, and end the worship of many forms of the deity. They also discouraged the practice of astrology and other rituals. Their preachings were in the Kannada language through devotional poetry, a language of the people. However, there were two sects in this group one who wanted the Sanskrit language to be followed, the Vyasakutaand the Dasakuta. The notable Haridasas of that period were Purandaradasa, Vyasaraya, Kanakadasa, Vadiraja, Vijaya Dasa, Jagannatha

Dasa, Vasudeva Dasa and Gopala Dasa; many of them became heads of the religious *maths* founded by Madhva and his disciples. Haridasas are still popular and the songs scripted by many of the earlier Haridasas are very popular.

Language

Talagunda Pillar inscription dates to the 5th century.

Karnataka is one of the four states of South India where Kannada is spoken. It is an ancient language of the Dravidian genre. Spread of Sanskrit in South India as a basic Hindu religious language is evidenced in a stone pillar inscription dated between 455 and 470 AD in Talagunda in Shivamogga district of the state. The inscription is in the language of Kadamba Kakusthavarman; the posthumous record is inscribed in Late southern Brahmi script during the reign of Santivarman (450 to 470 AD). Traditions of Hinduism are practiced in both Sanskrit (considered a superior language) and vernacular languages. The upper castes practice the religion mostly in Sanskrit, whereas the lower-class people practice it in the vernacular language of the region, which constitutes almost 80% of the rural community.

Castes

During the British Raj the caste classification of the Hindu religion, in their proper hierarchical order, was done in the late 19th century and a publication titled *Castes and Tribes of Southern India* was published. This monumental work covers all castes in all the states of the then British India; the Bombay state covered the region from Sind in the north (now in Pakistan) to Mysore State (now Karnataka) in the south.

Architecture

Chalukya dynasty

Left: Hoysaleswara Temple at Halebidu; Right: Virupaksha Temple, Hampi.

One of the seven rivers of India sacred to Hindus is the Kaveri River which has its origin in Karnataka and there are many Hindu tirtha sthanas (sacred sites or places) on its banks. One of the notable thirtha sthanas (religious centre) on the bank of the river is Srirangapattana. The historical site of Aihole is where the Chalukya dynasty ruled in the state from 4th-8th century. They built a large number of Hindu temples, some of which are still extant. This was the period of evolution of Hindu architecture. The architectural style introduced during this period were rock cut architecture in the form of cave temples (chaitya) which comprised an enclosed courtyard called vihara. The earliest temple built was in 450AD which had a square mandapa (pavilion) and a tower (shikara) above the image of the main deity. These became forerunners for later period Hindu temples and resulted in the evolution of Hindu medieval temple architecture.

Hoysala Empire

Th reign of the Hoysala Empire occurred between the 10th and 14th centuries over the western region of Karnataka. Many temples were built with chlorite stones or soapstones and the architecture which evolved was called the Hoysala architecture, known for architectural detailing.

The unique features of this style comprise a central hall linked to three star shaped shrines, and the temple towers are laid in horizontal tiers. Dorasamudra, known as Halebid, was the dynastic capital.

Hoysaleswara Temple is dedicated to the Hindu god Shiva as the family deity of the Hoysalas. Bittiga, the ruler of the Hoysala empire, converted from Jainism to Hinduism. He was given the name Vishnuvardhana by Ramanuja, one of the three eminent social reformers and religious heads of Hinduism who consecrated the Hoysaleswara Temple built in 1121.

Dedicated to Shiva, it has two sanctum sanctorums and the deities are in the form of lingas named Hoysaleshvara and Shantaleshvara, after the king and queen. Built over a period of 70 years, it was left incomplete. It has an enormous Nandi, the mount of Shiva. There is a small Surya (Sun god) temple behind the sanctorum deified with a Surya (Sun) image which is 2 metres (6 ft 7 in) in height. The walls of the temple have been carved with scenes of Ramayana, Mahabharata and the Bhagavad Gita epics; they are crafted on the external and internal walls, with Yabancharya named as the architect. The town was ravaged by Muslim invaders in 1327.

Left: Sculpture of Shiva's mount, Nandi, in Haleedu, Karnataka. Depictions of Nandi are common in the state; Right: Shiva tearing an elephant (Gajasura) - Chennakesava temple, Belur. Hoysala Empire architecture in Belu.

Vijayanagara Empire

Vijayanagara Empire ("city of victory") was founded by Harihara in 1336. During the invasion by Bahmani Sultanate (Muslim rulers), Harihara was captured and was converted to Islam, thus becoming an outcast among Hindu religionists. As he grew up, he became a valiant warrior and was sent to conquer South India for the Sultanate. But he decided to establish his own kingdom and reconverted to Hinduism, an indication of religious tolerance that was prevalent during the medieval period; there was no opposition from the orthodoxy. Hampi is another great city of the medieval period where the Vijayanagara empire flourished between 1336 and 1565 and held sway over most of the Indian peninsula; this city was sacked by the invading Muslim army in 1365.

9

Art, Architecture, Fair and Festivals

ART AND CULTURE OF KARNATAKA

The southern state of Karnataka, in India, has a distinct art and culture. The diverse linguistic and religious ethnicity that are native to state of Karnataka combined with their long histories cultural heritage of the state. Apart from Kannadigas, Karnataka is home to Tuluvas, who also consider themselves as Kannadigas. Minor populations of Tibetan Buddhists and Siddhi tribes plus a few other ethnic groups also live in Karnataka. The traditional folk arts e major theatrical forms of coastal Karnataka. Contemporary theatre culture in Karnataka is one of the most vibrant in India with organizations like Ninasam, Ranga Shankara and Rang on foundations laid down by the Gubbi Veeranna Nataka Company. Veeragase, Kamsale and Dollu Kunitha are popular dance forms. Bharatanatya also enjoys wide patronage in Karnataka.

Music

Karnataka is the only Indian state where both Hindustani and Carnatic singers flourish. North Karnataka is predominantly famous for Hindustani music and South Karnataka is well known for Carnatic music.

Carnatic

With the rise of Vaishnavism and the Haridasa movement came Karnataka composers like Purandaradasa, whose Kannada language works were lucid, devotional and philosophical and hence appealing to the masses. Other haridasas of medieval times were Kanakadasa, Vyasatirtha, Jayatirtha, Sripadaraya, Vadirajatirtha etc., who composed several *devara nama*. One of the earliest and prominent composers in South India was the saint, and wandering bard of yore Purandara Dasa. Though historians claim Purandara Dasa composed 75,000 - 475,000 songs in Sanskrit and Kannada, only a few hundred of them are known today. He was a source of inspiration to the later composers like Tyagaraja. Owing to his contribution to the Carnatic Music he is referred to as the *Father of Carnatic Music* (*Karnataka Sangeeta Pitamaha*). Purandaradasa codified and consolidated the teaching of Carnatic music by evolving several steps like *sarali, jantai(Janti), thattu varisai (Thattu Varise), alankara* and *geetham (geethe)* and laid down a framework for imparting formal training in this art form. Later in the 17th and 18th centuries, the haridasa movement would once again contribute to music in Karnataka in the form of haridasas such as Vijaya Dasa, Gopaladasa, Jagannathadasa who are just a few among a vast galaxy of devotional saints.

Hindustani

Karnataka has achieved a prominent place in the world of Hindustani music as well. Several of Karnataka's Hindustani musicians won the Kalidas Sanman, Padma Bhushan and Padma Vibhushan awards. Some famous performers are Gangubai Hangal, Puttaraj Gawai, Pt. Bhimsen Joshi, Pt. Mallikarjun Mansur, Basavaraj Rajguru, Sawai Gandharva and Kumar Gandharva.

Dance

Yakshagana

Yakshagana a form of dance drama is one of the major theatrical forms in coastal Karnataka. A fusion of folk and classical tradition makes Yakshagana a unique form of art which includes colourful costumes, music, dance, singing, and most importantly dialogs composed on the fly. Award-winning performers include Shambhu Hegde, Chittani Ramachandra Hegde. Yakshagana and Dollu Kunitha are two of the popular dance forms of Karnataka. Gamaka is a unique music form based on Karnakata Sangeetha.

Painting

The Bengal , along with the general influence of Ravi Varma school of painting, influenced the Mysore school of painting. King Krishnaraja Wodeyar III patronised famous painters including Sundarayya, Tanjavur Kondayya and Alasinrayya. King Krishnaraja Wodeyar IV patronised K. Venkatappa, Keshavayya, Y. Nagaraju, Y. Subramanya Raju, Paavanje, and Kamadolli. The Chamarajendra Technological Institute (CTI—currently modified into Chamarajendra Academy of Visual Arts—CAVA), Jaganmohan Art Gallery and Venkatappa Art Gallery are reminders of this heyday. Chitrakala Parishat is an organisation in Karnataka dedicated to promote visual arts, particularly the folk and traditional art.

Utsav Rock Garden which is located in Gotagodi Village, Shiggaon Taluk, Haveri District, Karnataka. It includes innumerable sculptures depicting the rural life of Karnataka and also a wide array of creative and modern paintings.

ARCHITECTURE OF KARNATAKA

The antiquity of Architecture of Karnataka can be traced to its southern Neolithic and early Iron Age, Having witnessed the architectural ideological and utilitarian transformation from shelter- ritual- religion. Here the nomenclature 'Architecture' is as old as c.2000 B.C.E. The upper or late Neolithic people in order to make their shelters, they constructed huts made of wattle and doab, that were buttressed by stone boulders, presumably having conical roof resting on the bamboo or wooden posts into red murram or paved granite chips as revealed in archaeological excavations in sites like Brhamagiri (Chitradurga district), Sanganakallu, Tekkalakota (Bellary district), Piklihal

(Raichur district). Megaliths are the dominant archaeological evidence of the early Iron Age (c. 1500 B.C.E- 100 C.E unsettled date). There are more than 2000 early Iron Age burial sites on record, who laid the foundation for a high non perishable architecture in the form of various distinct architectural styles of stone built burials, which are ritualistic in its character. The active religious architecture is evident 345 with that of the Kadamba Dynasty. Karnatakais a state in the southern part of India originally known as the State of Mysore. Over the centuries, architectural monuments within the region displayed a diversity of influences, often relaying much about the artistic trends of the rulers of twelve different dynasties. Its architecture ranges dramatically from majestic monolith, such as the Gomateshwara, to Hindu and Jain places of worship, ruins of ancient cities, mausoleums and palaces of different architectural hue. Mysore Kingdom (Wodeyar) rule has also given an architectural master structure in the St. Philomena's Church at Mysore (extolled by the King as a structure of divine compassion and the eager gratitude of men) which was completed in 1956, in addition to many Dravidian style architectural temples. Two of the monuments (Pattadakal and Hampi) are listed under the UNESCO World Heritage List of 22 cultural monuments in India. Styles of Indo-Saracenic, Renaissance, Corinthian, Hindu, Indo-Greek and Indo-British style palaces were built in Mysore, the city of palaces. Sikh architecture at Bidar (1512) and also in Bangalore in 1956 can also be cited as having an impact on the architectural composition of the state.

Apart from the ancient traditional Buddhist Viharas which existed in India since ancient times, since the Independence of India in 1947, Karnataka has experienced some marked architectural changes, notably by the influx of Tibetan refugees which arrived in the state between 1963 and 1997, bringing with them the traditional Tibetan art and architectural styles, reflected in the Buddhist monastery at Bylakuppe for instance. Vidhana Soudha (built in Bangalorein 1953) and the tallest temple at Murudeshwar are witnesses to the Neo–Dravidian architectural influences which have evolved since independence.

The chronology of the architecture of Karnataka is elaborated in the right-hand box.

Kadamba architecture

The Kadambas of Banavasi were the ancient royal dynasty of Karnataka from 345 to 525, and made a significant early contribution to the architectural heritage of Karnataka. Dr. G. M. Moraes opines that apart from using some unique features, the Kadambas incorporated a diversity of styles in their architecture (Kadamba architecture), derived from their predecessors and overlords, drawing upon the architectural tradition of the Satavahanas for instance. The Kadambas were the originators of the Karnataka architecture. The most prominent basic feature of their architecture is the Shikara (dome), called Kadamba Shikara. The Shikara is pyramid shaped and rises in steps without any decoration, with a stupika or kalasha at the top. Occasionally the pyramids had perforated screen windows. This style of Shikara was used several centuries later, having an influence on the Doddagaddavalli Hoysala Temple and the Mahakuta temples in Hampi. The Madhukeshwara (Lord Shiva) Temple in Banavasi was built by Kadambas, and has an intricately carved stone cot.Originally built by the Kadambas, it has undergone, over a period of a thousand years, many additions and renovations, from the Chalukyas to the rulers of Sonda. "Kadambotsava", an annual cultural festival is held here in the month of December.

Dravidian architecture

Cave temples and surface structural temples. Blend of North Indian Nagara style and South Indian Dravidian style

Various temples in the Jaina, Shaiva and Vishnu traditions were built under the Western Ganga Sovereign Dynasty, which was subordinate to Pallava from 350 to 550, under Chalukya overlordship until 753 and under Rashtrakuta overlordship until 1100. The construction of monuments such as Gomateshwara (982 – 983) in places such as Shravanabelagola, Kambadahalli and Talakadu by the Western Ganga kings reflect a tolerance to different faiths. Some Vaishnava temples were built by the Gangas, such as the Narayanaswami temples in Nanjangud, Sattur and Hangala, in the modern Mysore district.

Nanjangud temple originally built by the Ganga Dynasty rulers in the ninth century

Gomateshwara

Gomateshwara (983), situated in Shravanabelagola is a monolithic statue standing 17.8 metres (58 ft) high above a hill (618 steps climb leads to this monolith), and is visible from a distance of 30 kilometres (19 mi) and regarded as one of the largest monolithic statues in the world. The statue was built by the Ganga minister and commander Chavundaraya (940–989) in honour of Lord Bahubali. Carved from fine-grained white granite, the image stands on a lotus. It has no support up to the thighs and is 60 feet (18 m) tall with the face measuring 6.5 feet (2.0 m). With the serene expression on the face of the image, its curled hair with graceful locks, its proportional anatomy, the monolith size, and the combination of its artistry and craftsmanship have led it to be called the mightiest achievement in sculptural art in medieval Karnataka. It is the largest monolithic statue in the world.

Panchakuta basadi (Jain basadi)

This is one of the most elegant monuments built in Dravidian, Vesara and Nagara styles during the period between 900 and 1000. The temple, which is oriented to the north towards the Brahmadeva pillar, has five shrines (hence the name Panchakuta). Three shrines are connected to a mantapa by a vestibule and consist of the main shrine of tirthankara Adinatha flanked by Neminatha shrine to the east and Shanthinatha shrine containing a 3 metres (9.8 ft) tall idol of the tirthankara to the west. The other two shrines, which are disconnected and lie to the north of the trikuta cluster (three shrines), are also dedicated to tirthankaras. These are two different monuments.

Talakad

Talakad is a historical site along the banks of the Cauvery River near Mysore. This small town, with a strong history and a prolonged period of human settlement was a flourishing city during the Hoysala period (12th–13th century), and was also an important trade centre during the reign of Gangas (from the 6th century for about 400 years) and Cholas (close of 10th century) and the Hoysalas from 1116. Towards the early 15th century it came under the Vijayanagara rule, and remained with them until the end of the 16th century. There are about a dozen temples spread over a small area of 4 square kilometres (1.5 sq mi), perhaps reflecting the rich art, culture, trade and human activities that once existed there. The town now looks abandoned, except during the time of pilgrimage held once every few years. The temples, whose deities are regularly worshipped, such as the Kirthinarayana Temple, are either uncovered frequently or are protected continuously from accumulation of sand. The sand is removed to uncover them for a specific worship and an important pilgrimage held every five to twelve years; the recent Panchalinga Darshana pilgrimage was held during December 2006.

Nanjangud Temple

The temple, located at Nanjangud on the right bank of the Kabini River, was originally built in Dravidian style by the Ganga Dynastyrulers in the 9th century during their occupation of this region. It has undergone extensions during the reign of Cholas, Hoysalas, and Wodeyars from the 9th to 19th centuries. It is one of the biggest temples in Karnataka with an area of 560 square feet (52 m) and with a Gopura (tower) of 36.576 metres (120.00 ft) height, which has seven stories with seven gold plated Kalasas on top of the Gopura.

The uniqueness of the temple is that it has 66 idols of Shaiva saints called as Nayanmars and more than 100 Lingas (of different kinds and sizes) including the main deity of Srikanteshwara (Nanjundeshwara) Linga. The main deity is also called *Hakim Nanjundeswara*; a title given by Tippu Sultan. It is inscribed in the temple history that on Tippu Sultan's special prayers to the deity, eyesight of the royal elephant was restored, where after the Sultan had a lingam made of jade along with an emerald necklace and donated it to the temple.

Badami Chalukya architecture

The architecture is of a temple building idiom that evolved in the time period of 5th to 8th centuries in the area of Malaprabha basin, in present-day Bagalkot district of Karnataka state, sometimes called the Vesara style and Chalukya style. The earliest temples dating back to around 450 in Aihole when the Badami Chalukyas were feudatories of the Kadambas of Banavasi are also reflected during this period. According to historians, the Badami Chalukya contribution to temple building matched their valour and their achievements in battle. Their style included two types of monuments, namely the rock cut halls (caves) or cave temple features and the surface structural monuments.

Durga temple at Aihole North Karnataka

Cave temples

Cave temple architecture is found in the Badami cave temples at Badami, the early Chalukya capital, carved out in the 6th century. There are four cave temples hewn from the sides of cliffs, three Hindu and one Jain, which contain carved architectural elements such as decorative pillars and brackets as well as finely carved sculpture and richly etched ceiling panels. Nearby are many small Buddhist cave shrines. The four caves are simple in style. The entrance is a simple verandah with stone columns and brackets -a distinctive feature of these caves-leading to a columned mandapa and then to the small square shrine (sanctum sanctorum) cut deep into the cave. The temple caves represent different religious sects. Among them, two are dedicated to Lord Vishnu, one to Lord Shiva and the fourth is a Jain temple. The first three are devoted to the Vedic faith and the fourth cave is the only Jain temple at Badami.

The cave temples architecture is a blend of North Indian Nagara Style and South Indian Dravidian style. Each cave has a sanctum sanctorum, a mandapa, a verandah and pillars. The cave temples also bear exquisite carvings, sculpturesand beautiful murals

Western Chalukya architecture

Someshwara temple at Lakshmeshwara

Western Chalukya architecture , also known as Kalyani Chalukya or Later Chalukya architecture, is the distinctive style of ornamented architecture in the Shaiva, Vaishnava, and Jain religious traditions that evolved during the rule of the Western Chalukya Empire in the Tungabhadra region of central Karnataka, in the 11th and 12th centuries. Western Chalukyan political influence was at its peak in the Deccan Plateau during this period. The centre of cultural and temple building activity lay in the Tungabhadra region, where large medieval workshops built numerous monuments.These monuments, regional variants of pre-existing Dravida (South Indian) temples, defined the *Karnata dravida* tradition.

Temples of all sizes built by the Chalukyan architects during this era remain today, known as a transitional style and provides an architectural link between the style of the early Chalukya dynasty and that of the later Hoysala Empire.

Lakkundi temples

Lakkundi in Gadag district is a tiny village on the way to Hospet from Hubli. It is one of the fine architectural feasts of the Kalyana Chalukya period (about 10th century). Currently Lakkundi has about 50 temples of various stature and antiquity. All the temples are made of green schist and the outer walls and entrances are very richly decorated. The shikhara is an in-between-style type and the parapet and the artistic division of the wall with pilasters is typical of the south-Indian style. It is also known for Step wells and historic inscriptions. The centre of cultural and temple building activity lay in the Tungabhadra region, where large medieval workshops built numerous monuments. These monuments, regional variants of pre-existing Dravida (South Indian) temples, defined the Karnataka Dravida tradition.

Kashivisvanatha Temple

A great deal of care has gone into the construction of the Kashivisvanatha Temple in Lakkundi, which deifies Shiva. This temple has a unique feature: a small Surya (Sun) shrine faces the main shrine on the west. There is a common platform between both, which must have been an open mandapa originally. Hence, the Kashivisvanatha Temple has an entrance on the east side and south side of the mandapa. The entrance doorway and the towers are covered with close intricate carvings. The shikhara (dome) is in the North-Indian style and it looks like a lathe must have been used to make the complex circular pillars.

Brahma Jainalaya

Brahma Jaina Basti built by queen Attimabbe is the largest and oldest of many Jain temples in Lakkundi. This temple is dedicated to Mahavira, the most revered saint of Jainism. The temple has a garbhagriha shrine and mandapa style with deep beams on the mandapa from where the eaves are cantilevered.

The large Jaina temple, among the many temples at Lakkundi, also near Gadag, is perhaps one of the earliest examples of temples in this area built of a kind of fine-textured chloritic schist as distinct from the hitherto-used sandstone of this region.

The new material, because of its less thick quarry-sizes and tractability, reacted on the workmanship, with the result that the masonry-courses became reduced in size and the carvings more delicate and highly finished. The temple, perhaps built in the latter half of the 11th century, has a five-storeyed vimana (tower), square on plan from the base to the shikhara, and had originally a closed square navaranga in front, though an open mandapa was added in front later on. The central bay of the navaranga is a larger square than the peripheral eight around it. The second storey, as in the Jaina temple at Pattadakkal, is functional and has an antarala-mantapa in front over the vestibule of the lower storey. This raises the total height of the vimana considerably.

Mahadeva Temple

Mahadeva Temple at Itagi in the Koppal district, built in 1112, is an example of Dravida articulation with a nagara superstructure, dedicated to Shiva and is among the larger temples built by the Western Chalukyas and perhaps the most famous. Inscriptions hail it as the 'Emperor among temples'. Here, the main temple, the sanctum of which has a *linga*, is surrounded by thirteen minor shrines, each with its own *linga*. The temple has two other shrines, dedicated to Murthinarayana and Chandraleshwari, parents of Mahadeva, the Chalukya commanders who consecrated the temple in 1112.

Hoysala architecture

The Hoysala architecture style is an offshoot of the Western Chalukya style, which was popular in the 10th and 11th centuries. It is distinctively Dravidian, and owing to its unique features, Hoysala architecture qualifies as an independent style. The Hoysala sculpture in all its richness is said to be a challenge to photography. The artistry of the Hoysalas in stone has been compared to the finesse of an ivory worker or a goldsmith. The abundance of jewellery worn by the sculpted figures and the variety of hairstyles and headdresses depicted give a fair idea of the lifestyles of the Hoysala times.

Some of the famous temples of the Hoysala architectural style are the Kesava Temple at Somanathapura, Chennakesava Temple at Belur, Chikkamagalur Amruthapura Temple, Chennakesava Temple at Aralaguppe, the Hoysaleswara Temple at Halebidu, Cheluvanarayana Swamy Temple at Melkote.

Somanathapura

Somanathapura is famous for the Chennakesava Temple (also called Kesava or Keshava Temple) built by Soma, a dandanayaka (commander) in 1268 under Hoysala king Narasimha III, when the Hoysalas were the major power in South India. The Keshava Temple is one of the finest examples of Hoysala architecture and is in a very well preserved condition. Somnathpur, however, is truly unique in design, perfect in symmetry and the stone carvings are remarkable marvels in stone.

Chennakesava Temple at Belur

The Chennakesava Temple at Belur, originally called Vijayanarayana Temple, built on the banks of the Yagachi

River in Belur, an early capital of the Hoysala Empire, is one of the finest examples of Hoysala architecture. It was built by king Vishnuvardhana in commemoration of his victory over the Cholas at Talakad in 1117. The facade of the temple is filled with intricate sculptures and friezes with no portion left blank. Inside the temple are a number of ornate pillars. The temple is about 30 metres (98 ft) in height and has an impressive entrance gopuram (tower), built in Dravidian style. A group of subsidiary shrines surround the main shrine in the centre of a rectangular navaranga (hall). The navaranga (hall) supported by forty-six pillars, each of a different design, has three entrances guarded by decorated doorkeepers.

Hoysaleswara Temple

The Hoysaleswara Temple at Halebidu, was built by Ketamala and attributed to Vishnuvardhana. The temple complex comprises two Hindu temples, the Hoysaleshawara and Kedareshwara temples and two Jain basadis. It enshrines Hoysaleswara and Shantaleswara, named after the temple builder Vishnuvardhana Hoysala and his wife, Queen Shantala.

The Hoysaleswara Temple, dating back to the 1121, is astounding for its wealth of sculptural details. The temple is a simple dvikuta vimana (two-shrined), one for "Hoysaleswara" and the other for "Shantaleswara" (after Shantala Devi, queen of king Vishnuvardhana) and is built with chloritic chist (also known as soapstone). The temple complex as a whole is elevated on a jagati (platform), a feature that became popular in contemporary Hoysala designs. The walls of the temple are covered with an endless variety of depictions from Hindu mythology, animals, birds and *Shilabalikas* or dancing figures. Yet no two sculptures of the temple are the same. This magnificent temple guarded by a Nandi Bull was never completed, despite 86 years of labour. The temple of Halebidu, has been described as an "outstanding example of Hindu architecture" and as the "supreme climax of Indian architecture".

Ishvara Temple

The Ishvara Temple in Arasikere, dates to 1220 rule of Hoysala Empire. Arasikere (*lit* "Queens tank"; 'Arasi' means "queen" or "princess" and 'kere' means "tank" in the Kannada language). The temple, though modest in size and figure sculpture, is considered the most complex in architecture among surviving Hoysala monuments because of its ground plan: a 16-pointed star shaped mantapa (hall), in addition to an asymmetrical star shaped shrine, whose star points are of three different types.

The temple, which faces east like all Hoysala constructions, uses soapstone as basic building material and is a *ekakuta*shrine (single shrine or cella) with two *mantapas*, one open and one closed. All three units are connected to form a unity.The elegantly decorated ceilings, the domical ceiling of the open *mantapa*, the sculptures of Dwarapalakas (door keepers) in the closed *mantapa* (also called *navaranga*), the wall panel images numbering 120 (on pilasters between aedicules–miniature towers) carved on the outer walls are noteworthy.

Melkote Cheluvanarayana Swamy Temple

The Cheluvanarayana Swamy Temple, located in Melkote built on rocky hills is a square building of large dimensions but very plain, dedicated to Lord *Cheluva-Narayana Swamy* or Tirunarayana. Mysore Archaeological Department states, on the strength of epigraphic evidence, that the presiding deity of this temple was already a well known idol of worship before Sri Ramanujacharya, the Srivaishnava saint worshipped at the shrine in December 1098 and even before he came to the Mysore region and that very probably he used his influence to rebuild or renovate the temple. The temple is richly endowed, having been under the special patronage of the Mysore Wodeyars, and has a most valuable collection of jewels.

Lakshminarasimha Swamy Temple

The Lakshminarasimha Swamy Temple is a good example of a richly decorated Hoysala temple built in the trikuta (three towers) vimana (prayer hall) style with fine sculptures adorning the walls. The material used is Chloritic Schist (Soapstone) and the temple is built on a *jagati* (platform) that closely follows the plan of the temple. This is a Hoysala innovation. The Jagati is in perfect unity with the rest of the temple and the temple is built on a jagati (platform) that closely follows the plan of the temple. The size of the original temple can be considered small, to which a larger open mantapa (hall) was later added. The three shrines are located around a central closed mantapa with 9 bays. The ceiling of the closed *mantapa* is supported by four lathe turned pillars and is deeply domed in the centre. The ceiling of the closed mantapa is supported by four lathe turned pillars and is deeply domed in the centre. The central shrine is the most prominent and has a large tower. This shrine has a vestibule that connects the shrine to the mandapa. Consequently, the vestibule also has a tower that looks like an extension of the main tower and is called the sukanasi or nose. The other two shrines have smaller towers and because they have no vestibule to connect them to the central mantapa, they have no sukanasi.

Vijayanagara architecture

Vijayanagara architecture is a vibrant combination of the Chalukya, Hoysala, Pandya and Chola styles, idioms that prospered in previous centuries.

Ruins of Hampi – UNESCO World Heritage Site Virupaksha Temple, Krishna Temple, Vittala Temple, Ugra Narasimha and Kodandarama Temple are some of the famous monuments of the Vijayanagar style.

Its legacy of sculpture, architecture and painting influenced the development of the arts long after the empire came to an end. Its stylistic hallmark is the ornate pillared Kalyanamantapa (marriage hall), Vasanthamantapa (open pillared halls) and the Rajagopura (tower). While the empire's monuments are spread over the whole of Southern India, nothing surpasses the vast open-air theatre of monuments at its capital at Vijayanagara, a UNESCO World Heritage Site.

In the 14th century the kings continued to build Vesara or Deccan style monuments but later incorporated dravida-style gopurams to meet their ritualistic needs. The Prasanna Virupaksha Temple (underground temple) of Bukka Raya I and the Hazare Rama Temple of Deva Raya I are examples of Deccan architecture. The varied and intricate ornamentation of the pillars is a mark of their work. At Hampi, though the Vitthala Temple is the best example of their pillared Kalyanamantapa style, the Hazara Ramaswamy Temple is a modest but perfectly finished example. A grand specimen of Vijayanagara art, the Vitthala Temple, took several decades to complete during the reign of the Tuluva kings.

Another element of the Vijayanagara style is the carving of large monoliths such as the Sasivekalu (mustard) Ganesha and Kadalekalu (Ground nut) Ganesha at Hampi, the Gomateshwara statues in Karkala and Venur, and the Nandi bull in Lepakshi. The Vijayanagara Temples of Bhatkal, Kanakagiri, Sringeri and other towns of coastal Karnataka, as well as Tadpatri, Lepakshi, Ahobilam, Tirupati and Srikalahasti in Andhra Pradesh, and Vellore, Kumbakonam, Kanchi and Srirangam in Tamil Nadu are examples of this style. Vijayanagara art includes wall-paintings such as Dashavathara (ten incarnations of Vishnu) and Girija Kalyana (marriage of Goddess Parvati) in the Virupaksha Temple at Hampi, the Shivapurana paintings (tales of Shiva) at the Virabhadra Temple at Lepakshi, and those at the Jain basadi (temple) and the Kamaskshi and Varadaraja Temple at Kanchi. This mingling of the South Indian styles resulted in a richness not seen in earlier centuries, a focus on reliefs in addition to sculpture that surpasses that previously in India. An aspect of Vijayanagara architecture that shows the cosmopolitanism of the great city is the presence of many secular structures bearing Islamic features. The concentration of structures like pavilions, stables and towers suggests they were for use by royalty.This harmonious exchange of architectural ideas must have happened during rare periods of peace between the Hindu and Muslimkingdoms. The "Great Platform" (Mahanavami dibba) has relief carvings in which the figures seem to have the facial features of central Asian Turks who were known to have been employed as royal attendants.

Archaeological Survey of India's recent excavations in Hampi have revealed a large number of palatial complexes and basements of several platforms including a large number of stone images, beautiful terracotta objects and stucco figures. Ceramics and variety of porcelain and inscribed Buddhist sculptures of 2nd–3rd century have also been unearthed.

Indo-Islamic architecture

Mosque (17th century) in the mausoleum complex Ibrahim Rauza at Bijapur

Islamic architecture in Karnataka evolved during the period of the Adil Shahi dynasty of Indian sultans and Bahamani kings who ruled the Sultanate of Bijapur (1490 to 1686); Gol Gumbaz is the most popular monument of this period.

Gol Gumbaz

Gol Gumbaz (Kannada: ಗೋಲ ಗುಮ್ಮಟ), of Indo Islamic architectural style, is the mausoleum of Mohammed Adil Shah (1626 – 1656). at Bijapur of the Adil Shahi dynasty of Indian sultans, who ruled the Sultanate of Bijapur from 1490 to 1686. The tomb, located in the city of Bijapur was built in 1659 by the famous architect, Yaqut of Dabul.

The construction of this building was completed and the deceased king was interred in this building in 1656 and contains the sepulcher containing the tombs of Muhammad Adil Shah, the seventh Sultan of the Adil Shahi dynasty, his wives and daughters.

The structure, built of grey basalt and decorated plaster, consists of a massive square chamber measuring nearly 50 metres (160 ft) on each side and covered by a huge dome 37.9 metres (124 ft) in diameter making it the second largest pre-modern dome in the entire world (after the dome of Hagia Sophia and Pantheon) with thickness varying from 3.05 metres (10.0 ft) near the base to 2.74 metres (9.0 ft) near the top, and has a floor area of 1,703.56 square metres (18,337.0 sq ft).

The dome is supported on giant squinches supported by groined pendentives while outside the building is supported by domed octagonal corner towers. The Dome is unsupported by any pillars.

The acoustics of the enclosed place make it a whispering gallery where even the smallest sound is heard across the other side of the Gumbaz.

Any whisper, clap or sound gets echoed around 10 times. Each tower consists of seven storeys, and the upper floor of each opens on to a round gallery which surrounds the dome. In the centre of the chamber is a square raised podium approached by steps in the centre of each side.

Keladi Nayaka art of the Nayaka kingdoms

Aghoreshwara Temple, Hoysala-Kadamba style

Rameshwara Temple at Keladi

The Keladi Nayakas (period: 1499 – 1763) built some fine temples in Ikkeri and Keladi using a combination of late Kadamba, Hoysala, Vijayanagara and Dravida styles. The use of granite for their construction shows that they simply followed the Vijayanagar model of architecture. The Aghoreshwara Temple at Ikkeri and the Rameshwara Temple at Keladi are the best examples of the Nayakas' art. Vijayanagar-style pillars with hippogryphs are common; called yali columns (depiction of horses and lions as seen in Hampi) is found here. These are pillars with lions, either with their forepaws raised or simply in a sitting position, and pillars with a mythical horse-like animal with front legs raised, balancing on its rear legs, and with an armed rider on its back. A roof sculpture depicting a Gandaberunda (see image in infobox), the mythical two-headed bird of Karnataka, symbol of the state, is found in Keladi.

Aghoreshwara Temple

At Ikkeri, in the citadel, a palace was built with mud and timber, adorned with carvings. Today what remains is the Aghoreshvara Temple (one of the several names of Lord Shiva), in Ikkeri (was the capital of Keladi Nayakas). It is a large and well proportioned stone-building, constructed in a mixed style with a unique conception. There are carvings and sculptures such as Temple Relief (sculpture consisting of shapes carved on a surface so as to stand out from the surrounding background), erotica, figurines, old Kannada Manuscript, sculpted elephant, etc. There are intricate carvings on the stone walls of the temple. Yalis sculpted on the pillars of the Aghoreswara and Rameshwara temples depict mythical lion and it has been widely used in south Indian sculpture. Description and references to yalis is very old, but its depiction in the south Indian sculpture became prominent from the 16th century as seen in the Nayaka period temples. Yalis are believed to be more powerful than the lion or the elephant.

The Rameshwara Temple at Keladi was built in the Hoysala-Dravida style. This temple is made of stone and is on the banks of the Tunga River. The sanctum sanctorum of the temple has a Lingam, which is said to have been installed by Sage Parashurama himself.

Architecture of Kingdom of Mysore

The Kingdom of Mysore was subordinate to Vijayanagara Empire until 1565 and princely state under the paramouncy of the British Raj after 1799. The architectural designs were in the Indo-Saracenic – blends of Hindu, Muslimor Islamic, Rajput, and Gothic styles of architecture under the Wodeyar Dynasty or Kingdom of Mysore from 1399 to 1947.

Indo-Saracenic type is most notably manifested in palaces and courtly buildings built in various styles, and temples built in the Dravidian style. It is the city of Mysore that is best known for its royal palaces, earning it the nickname "City of Palaces". The city's main palace, the Mysore Palace, was designed by the English architect Henry Irwin in 1897. The palace's exterior is Indo-Saracenic in style but the wealth of detail inside is distinctly of Hoysala. Domes, arches, colonnades and carved pillars, as well as its size, add to this palace's notability. The octagonal *Kalyana mantapa* (Marriage Hall) on the ground floor has 26 canvas paintings on its walls depicting the Dassera procession. On the first floor, a marble staircase leads to a grand colonnaded Durbar hall containing famous paintings, including one of the Hindu god Vishnu on the ceiling. The opulent Amba Vilas hall, with its carved teakwood ceiling, white marble floors, semi-precious inlay work in the Agra style, silver door with a depiction of the dashavatara and *dikpalas* (guardians), teak doors inlaid with ivory, Belgian stained glass, cast iron pillars from Glasgow, etched glass windows and chandeliers are worthy of mention.

Jaganmohan Palace, Hindu style

The other palaces in Mysore are:

The Lalitha Mahal Palace, built in 1921 by E.W. Fritchley in the architectural style Renaissance, exhibits concepts from English manor houses and Italian palazzos, with the central dome believed to have been modelled on St. Paul's Cathedral in London.

The Jaganmohan Palace, mostly in the Hindu style built in the middle of the 19th century noted for its ornamental pavilion (called the Wedding Pavilion), and has an elegant façade with three large entrances; the Jayalakshmi Vilas Palace built in the Corinthian style consisting of a three-winged building with two Corinthian and Ionic columns; the sculptures of the Hindu goddess Lakshmi on the north side and of the goddess Bhuvaneshwari on the south side are particularly notable.

The Karanji Vilas mansion (1932), an Indo-Greek style building; the Cheluvamba Mansion (1910)- an imposing yet balanced structure, its main façade contains twin towers flanking semi-circular columned verandas on the ground and first floors.

The Maharaja's summer palace (1880), is called the Lokaranjan Mahal that initially served as a school for royalty.

The Rajendra Vilas Palace (1938) is built in the Indo-British style atop the Chamundi Hill.

Other royal mansions built by the Mysore rulers were the Chittaranjan Mahal in Mysore and the Bangalore Palace in Bangalore, a structure built on the lines of England's Windsor Castle.

Surrounding the main palace in Mysore and inside the fort are five temples, built in various periods namely, the Prasanna Krishnaswamy Temple (1829), the Lakshmiramana Swamy Temple, the oldest of the fort temples (existed prior to 1499); the Trinesvara Swamy Temple, built for the three-eyed god Shiva, existed since the time of King Raja Wodeyar and was renovated by successive kings; the Shweta Varaha Swamy Temple is unique in that it contains many aspects of Hoysala architecture; and the Prasanna Venkataramana Swami Temple, a Vishnu temple containing 12 murals of the Wodeyar rulers, built by Subbaraya Dasa, an officer of Maharaja Krishnaraja Wodeyar III, in 1836.

Sikh architecture

Gurudwara on the bank of Ulsoor lake in Bangalore

The earliest Sikh Gurudwara in Karnataka is the Guru Nanak Jhira Sahib at Bidar. It was built in traditional Sikh architecture style, at a sacred place located at Bidar in Bidar District. It is also called Nanak Jhira, where Jhira means a spring of water exists. Legend says that Guru Nanak halted here on his way to Sri Lanka in 1512.

During that period, people of Bidar were suffering from shortage of drinking water. A fountain of cool water rose out from a hill by the spiritual power of Guru Nanak. A committee took up development work of Gurudwara Nanak Jhira Sahib with the central three-storey building completed in 1966, which encases the historic Nanak Jhira spring divined by Gurunanak. The water of the fountain is collected in 'Amrit-Khud' (a tank of potion), built in white marble. There is a Sikh museum, built in the memory of Guru Tegh Bahadur, depicting the important events of Sikh history through pictures and paintings. There is a Sikh museum, built in the memory of Guru Tegh Bahadur, depicting the important events of Sikh history through pictures and paintings. Built in the Sikh architecture style, the Gurdwara is a lively blend of the Mughal and Rajput styles. Onion-shaped domes, multi-foil arches, paired pilasters, in-lay work, frescoes, etc. are of Mughal extraction, more specially of Shah Jahan's period, while oriel windows, bracket supported eaves at the string-course, chattris, richly ornamented friezes, etc., are derived from elements of Rajput architecture such as is seen in Jaipur, Jodhpur, Bikaner and other places in Rajasthan.

Apart from the above ancient Gurudwara at Bidar, Bangalore city also has Gurudwaras dated to 20th century. Guru Nanak, the Sikh Guru, was the first Sikh to visit Bengaluru. On his way back from Sri Lanka he halted at Bangalore. Kempegowda, the builder of Bangalore, met him and sought his blessings. Gurunanak not only blessed Kempegowda but also told him to develop the place. But it took many more years for a Sikh Gurudwara to be built in Bangalore. There are now three Gurudwaras in Bangalore. The first Sikh Gurudwara and the largest in Bangalore near the Ulsoor Lake on the Kensington Road, is an elegant and white structure, which was opened on 13 April 1946. It has been renovated recently with marble floors.

Buddhist culture & architecture

While under the Mauryas and Satavahanas Buddhism prospered in Karnataka, the influence of Hinduism expanded as it subsumed most of the teachings of Buddha and Buddhism and thus Buddhism lost its distinct uniqueness in the state. However, in the 20th century, Buddha viharas have been established in the State with Bangalore recording two such viharas.

The Maha Bodhi Society (MBS) was established by Acharya Buddharakkhita in 1956 at Bangalore with the objective of propagating the teachings of the Buddha and to provide the inspiration and facilities for putting that teaching into practice through spiritual, social, educational activities. The first act of the Acharya was to plant a sampling of the holy Bodhi tree from Bodh Gaya at the premises of the proposed Society. This tree has grown with the Society and is venerated. The Maha Bodhi Society Temple, a relatively new structure, was then built with the main shrine replicating the historic tower at Bodh Gaya. Temple as built is a brick structure with a central tower of 55 m (180.4 ft) height. The Stupa that represents a basic factor in the teaching of the Buddha has also been built at the entrance to the temple, which is made of granite and it enshrines a relic of the Buddha. The temple, the stupa and the Bodhi tree in the temple complex now form a unique landmark in Bangalore. It is a place of worship and meditation, a centre of pilgrimage for people from all over India and other countries.

Tibetan Buddhist culture & architecture

Apart from the Indian Buddhist traditions in the form of Viharas seen in various parts of the country, Tibetan Buddhist monasteries have also made a lasting impact in Karnataka with the influx of refugees from Tibet who were settled in Bylakuppe. One of the famous monasteries is the Namdroling monastery, built as per traditional Tibetan architecture, which is located in Bylakuppe near Kushalnagar in Kodagu in Karnataka. This spectacular Tibetan Golden Temple is a major tourist spot in the area. It is termed the 'Charming mini Tibet near Madikeri'. Tibetan refugees have both recreated their lifestyle as well as adapted to the local conditions around the monasteries. Huge golden statues, bright coloured wall paintings all around, gigantic dragons on the pillars in a high and big hall are a sight to behold.

A lineage of Tibetan Buddhism in the world, the monastery is home to a sangha community of over five thousand lamas (both monks and nuns), a religious college (or shedra) and hospital. The monastery was established by Penor Rinpoche (construction started in 1963 and inaugurated in 1999).

Built in typical Tibetan architecture style with Chinese and Indian influences, the monastery reflects a deeply Buddhist approach. It has the Buddhist mandatory Prayer wheel, along with two deer or dragons, same as can be seen on nearly every Gompa in Tibet. Tibetan art, a form of sacred art, in the form of the exquisitely detailed statues to wooden carvings to the intricate designs of the Thangka paintings (a syncrestism of Chinese scroll-painting with Nepalese and Kashmiri painting) are seen in this monastery.

10

Education

INTRODUCTION

Indian Institute of Science is one of the premier institutes of India.

As per the 2011 census, Karnataka had a literacy rate of 75.36%, with 82.47% of males and 68.08% of females in the state being literate.

In 2001, the literacy rate of the state were 67.04%, with 76.29% of males and 57.45% of females being literate. The state is home to some of the premier educational and research institutions of India such as the Indian Institute of Science, the Indian Institute of Management, the Indian Institute of Technology Dharwad the National Institute of Mental Health and Neurosciences, the National Institute of Technology Karnataka and the National Law School of India University.

In March 2006, Karnataka had 54,529 primary schools with 252,875 teachers and 8.495 million students, and 9498 secondary schools with 92,287 teachers and 1.384 million students. There are three kinds of schools in the state, viz., government-run, private aided (financial aid is provided by the government) and private unaided (no financial aid is provided). The primary languages of instruction in most schools are Kannada and English.

The syllabus taught in the schools is either of the CBSE, the ICSE or the state syllabus (SSLC) defined by the Department of Public Instruction of the Government of Karnataka. However, some schools follow the NIOS syllabus. The state has two sainik schools — in Kodagu Sainik School in Kodagu and in Bijapur Sainik School in Bijapur.

To maximise attendance in schools, the Karnataka Government has launched a midday meal scheme in government and aided schools in which free lunch is provided to the students.

Statewide board examinations are conducted at the end of secondary education. Students who qualify are allowed to pursue a two-year pre-university course, after which they become eligible to pursue under-graduate degrees.

There are 481 degree colleges affiliated with one of the universities in the state, viz. Bangalore University, Gulbarga University, Karnatak University, Kuvempu University, Mangalore University and Mysore University. In 1998, the engineering colleges in the state were brought under the newly formed Visvesvaraya Technological University headquartered at Belgaum, whereas the medical colleges are run under the jurisdiction of the Rajiv Gandhi University of Health Sciences.

Some of these baccalaureate colleges are accredited with the status of a deemed university.

There are 186 engineering, 39 medical and 41 dental colleges in the state.

Udupi, Sringeri, Gokarna and Melkote are well-known places of Sanskrit and Vedic learning. In 2015 the Central Government decided to establish the first Indian Institute of Technologyin Karnataka at Dharwad. Tulu and Konkani languages are taught as an optional subject in the twin districts of South Canara and Udupi.

Manipal Academy Of Higher Education, PES University and Christ University are private universities in Karnataka.

High literacy districts

Rank	District	Literacy
1	Udupi	88.57%
2	Bangalore Urban	87.67%
3	Dakshina Kannada (South Canara)	86.24%
4	Uttara Kannada (North Canara)	84.06%
5	Kodagu	82.61%

High literacy taluks

Rank	Taluk	Literacy
1	Mangaluru (Dakshina Kannada)	92%
2	Karwar (Uttara Kannada)	90%
3	Udupi (Udupi)	89%
4	Madikeri (Kodagu)	88%
5	Sirsi (Uttara Kannada)	88%

EDUCATION IN KARNATAKA

The state of Karnataka in India has institutions like the Indian Institute of Science IISc, Indian Institute of Technology, Dharwad IIT, Indian Institute of Management IIM, the National Institute of Technology Karnataka NITK, Indian Institute of Information Technology, Dharwad IIIT, VVisvesvaraya Technological University VTU and the National Law School of India University. In addition, a Visvesvaraya Institute of Advanced Technology (VIAT) is being constructed in Muddenahalli.

As per the 2011 census, Karnataka has a literacy rate of 75.36% with 82.47% of males and 68.08% of females being literate.

Primary and secondary education

Pramati Hillview Academy, Mysore

As of March 2006, Karnataka had 54,529 primary schools with 252,875 teachers and 8.495 million students. Likewise, there are 9,499 secondary schools with 92,287 teachers with 1.384 million students.

There are three kinds of schools in Karnataka: government (run by the government), aided (financial aid is provided by the government), and unaided private (no financial aid is provided). In majority of these schools, the medium of instruction is either English or Kannada. The syllabus taught in the schools is that of CBSE, ICSE, NIOS, or the state syllabus (defined by the Department of Public Instruction of the Government of Karnataka). The curriculum includes subjects like science, social studies and mathematics apart from language-related subjects. To maximize attendance, the Karnataka Government has launched a midday meal scheme in government and aided schools in which free lunch is provided to the students.

At the end of secondary education, the students pursuing the state syllabus have to pass an examination called the Secondary School Leaving Certificate (SSLC) to move on to the next level. The SSLC is administered by the Karnataka Secondary Education Examination Board.

Pre-university education

Students who have passed the SSLC have to pursue a two-year pre-university course (PUC) or a three-year diploma course before they are granted admission to a degree (baccalaureate) college. In the pre-university course, the student has to choose one among the three streams of Arts, Commerce, and Science depending on the kind of degree the student wants to pursue later. The Arts stream includes subjects like History, Sociology and Political Science; the Commerce stream includes subjects like Accountancy, Economics and Business Mathematics; and the Science stream includes subjects like Physics, Chemistry, Mathematics, Biology, Electronics and computer science.

International schools and certification boards

Bengaluru is a city that caters to the needs of prospective parents seeking international education for their children. Bengaluru has evolved into a global education hubs due to its cosmopolitan residents. Most of the international schools follow IB (international baccalaureate, Geneva) or Cambridge (Cambridge International Examinations, Britain) curricula. (The ICSE and CBSE are the curricula followed by most of the Indian schools in Karnataka.)

These international schools focus more on holistic education and inquiry-based learning for their students than just focusing on rote learning.

Baccalaureate education

There are 481 degree colleges that are run under the jurisdiction of the universities in the state — Bangalore University, Kuvempu University, Mysore University, Mangalore University, Gulbarga University, and Karnatak University. Deemed universities such as Christ University, Manipal

University also exist. Apart from these, there is the Visvesvaraya Technological University which oversees many of the engineering colleges in the state.

The medical colleges in the state are run under the jurisdiction of the Rajiv Gandhi University of Health Sciences. Some of these baccalaureate colleges are accredited with the status of a deemed university which grants them independence in chalking out their own syllabus and awarding degrees on their own. There are 123 engineering, 35 medical, and 40 dental colleges in the state.

The state has two universities offering courses related to agriculture: the universities of Agricultural Sciences, Dharwad and University of Agricultural Sciences, Bangalore. The state has set up a Karnataka Veterinary, Animal and Fisheries Sciences University at Bidar.

Other universities established by the state government are Kannada University, Karnataka State Open University, and Karnataka Women University.

There is Manipal University which is private. Karnataka has many deemed universities like NITK, NIHMANS etc.

Technical education

The first engineering college (University Visvesvaraya College of Engineering, UVCE) in Karnataka was started by the then Diwan of Mysore Sir M. Visvesvaraya in 1917 in Bengaluru. It was the fifth engineering college to be started in the country. By 1956, Karnataka had two Government and three private engineering colleges in the state.

Bibliography

Atri, Ajit : *Gandhi's View of Legal Justice,* New Delhi, Deep and Deep Pub., 2007.

Barker, Amanda.*India.*Crystal Lake, Ill.: Ribgy Interactive Library, 1996.

Burman, J.J. Roy: *Gujarat Unknown : Hindu-Muslim Syncretism and Humanistic Forays,* Mittal, Delhi, 2005.

Coleman, James S. and Rosberg jr., Carl G.: *Political Parties and National Integration in Tropical Africa,* Berkely, 1964.

Cumming, David.*India.*New York: Bookwright, 1991.

Das, Prodeepta.*Inside India.*New York: F. Watts, 1990.

Gaur, Sanjay: *Narendra Modi : Change We can Believe In,* Yking Books, Delhi, 2014.

Gerald D.: *Determining Economic Damages,* Santa Ana, CA: James Publishing, 1995.

Ghoshal, U. N.: A *History of Indian Political Ideas.* London, 1966.

Greer, Douglas F.: *Industrial Organization and Public Policy,* MacMillan Publishing Company, 1992.

Gupta, L.C., M.C. Gupta, Anil Sinha and Vinod K. Sharma *Gujarat Earthquake 26 January, 2001,* Indian Institute of Public Administration, Delhi, 2002.

Hallgren, M. H., & McAdams, A. K.: *The Economic Efficiency of Internet Public Goods,* Massachusetts, MIT Press, 1997.

Harrigan, K. R.: *Strategies for Declining Businesses.* Lexington, MA: Heath, 1980

Hart, Oliver: *Firms, Contracts, and Financial Structure,* Clarendon Press, Oxford, 1995.

Hausman, D. M.: *The Inexact and Separate Science of Economics,* Cambridge, Cambridge University Press, 1992.

Hayek, F. A. *Individualism and Economic Order,* The University of Chicago Press, Chicago, 1948.

Huang, Chi-fu: *Foundations of Financial Economics,* Prentice-Hall, 1988.

Hunt, E. K. *History of Economic Thought, A Critical Perspective,* New York, HarperCollins, 1992.

Jack Kemp: *A Monetary Agenda for the World Economy,* Boston, Quantum, 1984.

Jain S.C. : *New Trends in Rural Marketing,* RBSA Pub, Delhi, 2011.

Jeffrey D. Jones: *Handbook of Business Valuation,* New York: Wiley, 1992.

Judith, E.: *The Sexual Exploitation of Panchayati Raj,* Cambridge, Polity Press, 1986.

Kalman, Bobbie.*India: The Culture.*Toronto: Crabtree Publishing Co., 1990.

Kamath, M.V. and Kalindi Randeri: *Narendra Modi : The Architect of A Modern State,* Rupa, Delhi, 2009.

Kamble, N. D.: *Deprived Castes and their Struggle for Equality,* Ashish Publishing House, New Delhi, 1983.

Kelly, F. P.: *Charging and Accounting for Bursty Connections,* Massachusetts, MIT Press, 1997.

Kieve, L.: *Urban Land Economics,* London, MacMillan Press, 1977.

Loomes, G.: *Current Issues in Microeconomics,* New York: St. Martin's Press, 1989.

Maheshwari, Shriram: *Rural Development in India: A Public Policy Approach,* New Delhi, Sage, 1995.

Marino, Andy: *Narendra Modi: A Political Biography,* HarperCollins, Delhi, 2014.

Martin, Gerald D.: *Determining Economic Damages,* Santa Ana, CA: James Publishing, 1995.

Mathur, Y. B.: *Women's Education in India 1813-1966,* Asia Publishing House, 1973.

Mazumder, Sukhendu : *Politico-Economic Ideas of Mahatma Gandhi : Their Relevance in the Present Day,* New Delhi, Concept Pub., 2004.

Mehta, Nalin and Mona G. Mehta: *Gujarat Beyond Gandhi: Identity, Conflict and Society,* Routledge, Delhi, 2011.

Menon, V. P.: *The Transfer of Power in India,* Bombay, Orient Longman, 1957.

Morris-Jones, W.H.: *The Government and Politics of India,* London, Hutchinson, 1971.

Pandian, Jacob.*The Making of India and Indian Traditions.*Englewood Cliffs, N.J.: Prentice Hall, 1995.

Index

L

M

P

R

S

T

U

V

W

www.ingramcontent.com/pod-product-compliance
Ingram Content Group UK Ltd.
Pitfield, Milton Keynes, MK11 3LW, UK
UKHW042015290726
14061UKWH00001BB/15

9 789388 318778